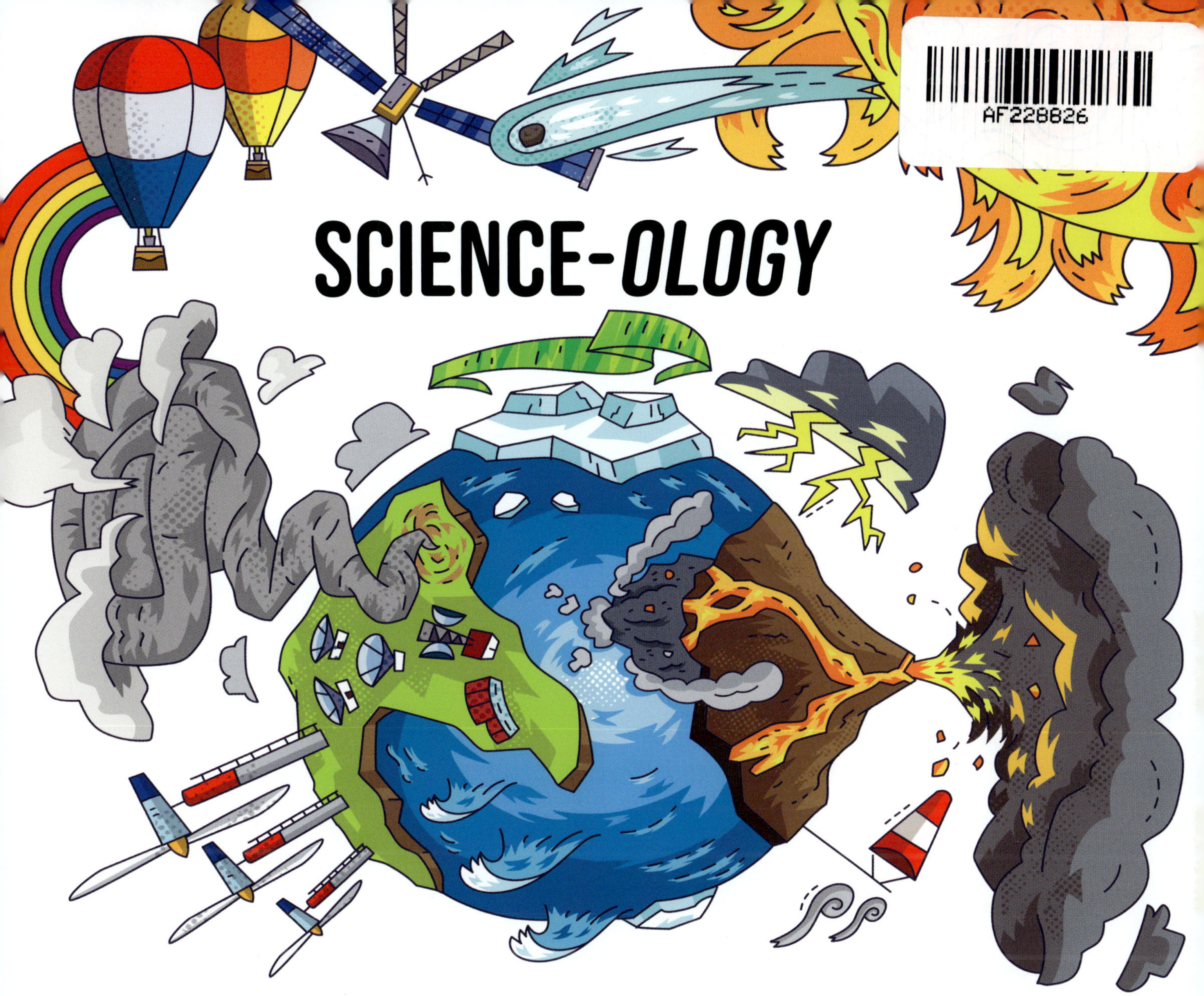

SCIENCE-*OLOGY*

METEOROLOGY

ANNA CLAYBOURNE
DANIEL LIMÓN

PowerKiDS press

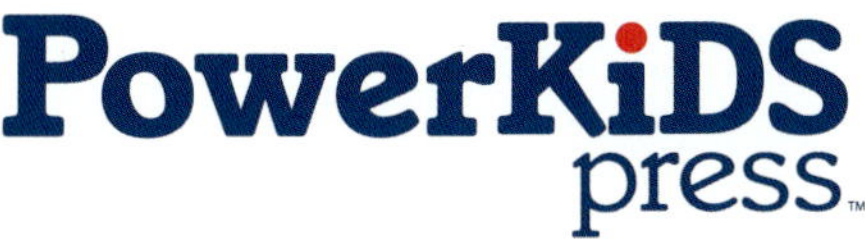

Published in 2026 by The Rosen Publishing Group, Inc.
2544 Clinton Street, Buffalo, NY 14224

First published in Great Britain in 2023 by Wayland
Copyright © Hodder and Stoughton, 2023

Editor: Elise Short
Consultant: Dr Ted Letcher, Research Physical Scientist at Cold Regions Research and Engineering Laboratory
Design: Rocket Design (East Anglia) Ltd
Illustrations: Daniel Limón

Cataloging-in-Publication Data
Names: Claybourne, Anna, author. | Limón, Daniel Sanchez, illustrator.
Title: Meteorology / by Anna Claybourne, illustrated by Daniel Limón.
Description: Buffalo, NY : PowerKids Press, 2026. |
  Series: Science-ology | Includes glossary and index.
Identifiers: ISBN 9781499454758 (pbk.) | ISBN 9781499454765 (library bound) |
  ISBN 9781499454772 (ebook)
Subjects: LCSH: Meteorology--Juvenile literature.
Classification: LCC QC863.5 C539 2026 | DDC 551.5--dc23

Picture credits: Alamy: ClassicStock 29t; Image China 42b; Pictorial Press 34b; Ariadne Van Zandbergen 42.
Dreamstime: Kurkal 12tr; Sergey Mashchenko 22tr.
iStock: Beyond images 33b; Rainer von Brandis 39b.
Iowa State University Alumni Association: 25t.
NASA:20t, 20b.
Shutterstock: Aerovista Luchfotographie 40b; And4me 27t; Aphelleon, elements furnished by NASA 4-5bc; AridOcean 36t; Fredy Bustamante 38-39; GG Digital arts 17b, 20t; Golden Sikorka 28bc; GoodStudio 37b; Hecke61 6bl; Hedgehog94 28bl; Maike Hildebrandt 23c; Iconic Bestiary 28br; Jorge 1984 Valencia 353t; Nick Julia 11t; K3Star 8t; Klyaksun 41br; LeManna 11b; Macrovector 17c, 23t, 28tl, 28tc, 28c; Irina Marchenko 45t; Mentalmind 45b; Mesa Studios. 37t; Metamorworks 30t; Miniaria 44t; ND700 11c; Peiyang 3c, 20t; John Rehg 4t, Rickt 28tr; Sensvector 32, 33l; John D Sirlin 24 main; Nadia Snopeck 4bl, 10t; Sunshine Vector 3br, 4cl, 6br; Tartila 34-35b; 3DBear 29b; Julia Tim 22tl; Vladimir Tretyakov 43t; Vega_7 41bl; Vladwel 9b;WinWin artlab 21b; Claudio Zaccherini 12tl; Ziablik 10c.
Image Courtesy of UW-Madison: 24 inset.
Wikimedia Commons: Hans Gros,1860-1924 9t; Kahnx 14c; Rijksmuseum CC0 1.0/PD;NASA.

Manufactured in the United States of America
CPSIA Compliance Information: Batch #CSPK26. For further information contact Rosen Publishing at 1-800-237-9932.

Find us on 

CONTENTS

A WHOLE WORLD OF WEATHER

Wherever you are in the world, at any time of the day or year, just step outside, and there it is – the weather!

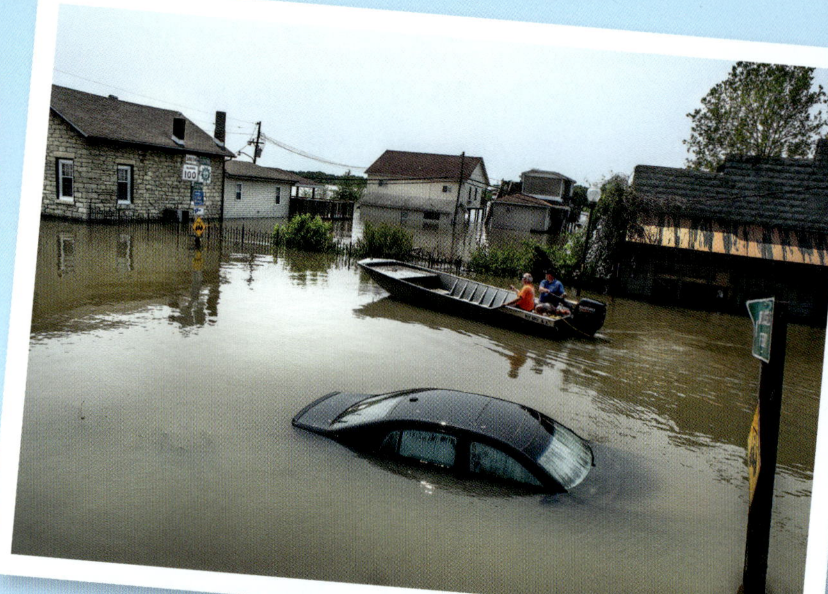

Weather can even be a matter of life or death, when a disaster, such as a flood or tornado, strikes. This car was washed away by a flood in Grafton, Illinois.

What's the weather doing today?

It's an old joke that people always chat about the weather. And they do! But that's because it's an incredibly important part of our lives.

Everyone on Earth is surrounded by endlessly changing weather: sunlight, heat and cold, moving air, and water falling from the sky. It affects what we wear, the activities and sports we do, where we can travel, the food farmers grow, and people's jobs, health, and happiness.

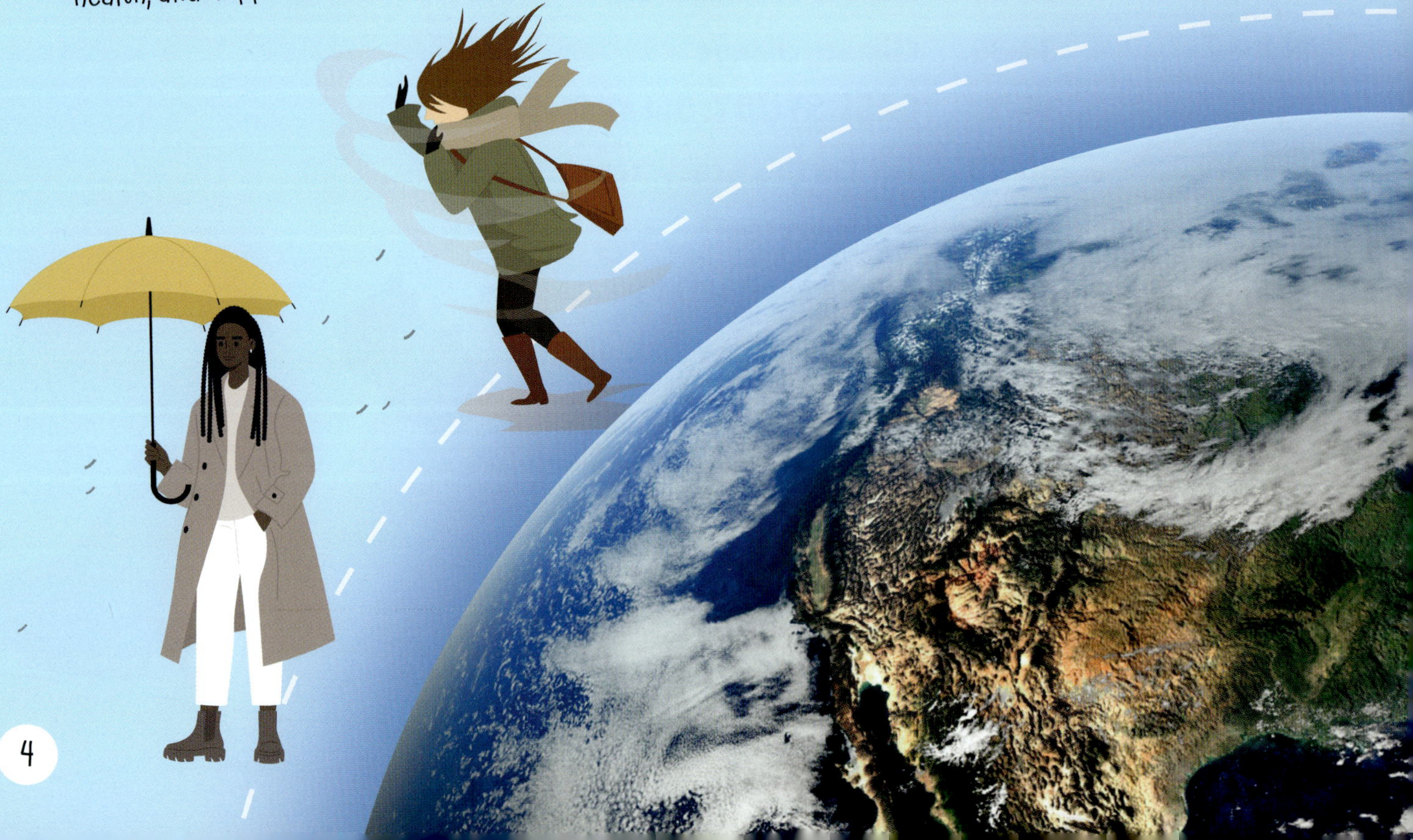

Weathery world

Weather happens because of the atmosphere, the layer of gases surrounding Earth. We need the atmosphere. It contains the air we breathe and helps to keep Earth's surface warm enough for life.

However, we can't control all the powerful forces that make the atmosphere swirl around, heat up, cool down, and create storms, droughts, or blizzards. All we can do is try to understand how the weather works, and predict what it will do next.

Ancient weather science

Humans have been trying to understand and predict the weather for thousands of years.

- Many ancient gods were weather gods, such as Asiaq, Inuit goddess of rain and snow.

- 3,000-year-old poems from ancient China describe how different clouds cause different weather.

- The ancient Greek philosopher, Aristotle, wrote a book called *Meteorologica* about the Earth and its weather around 340 BCE.

Scientists called meteorologists measure and study weather.

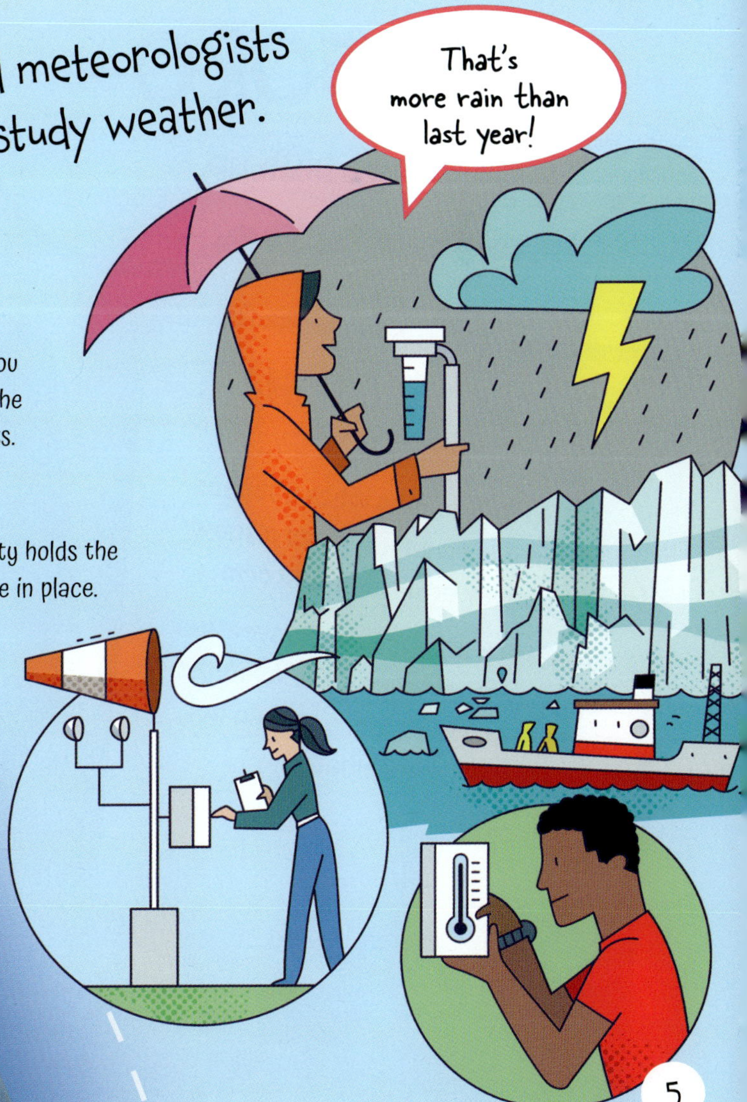

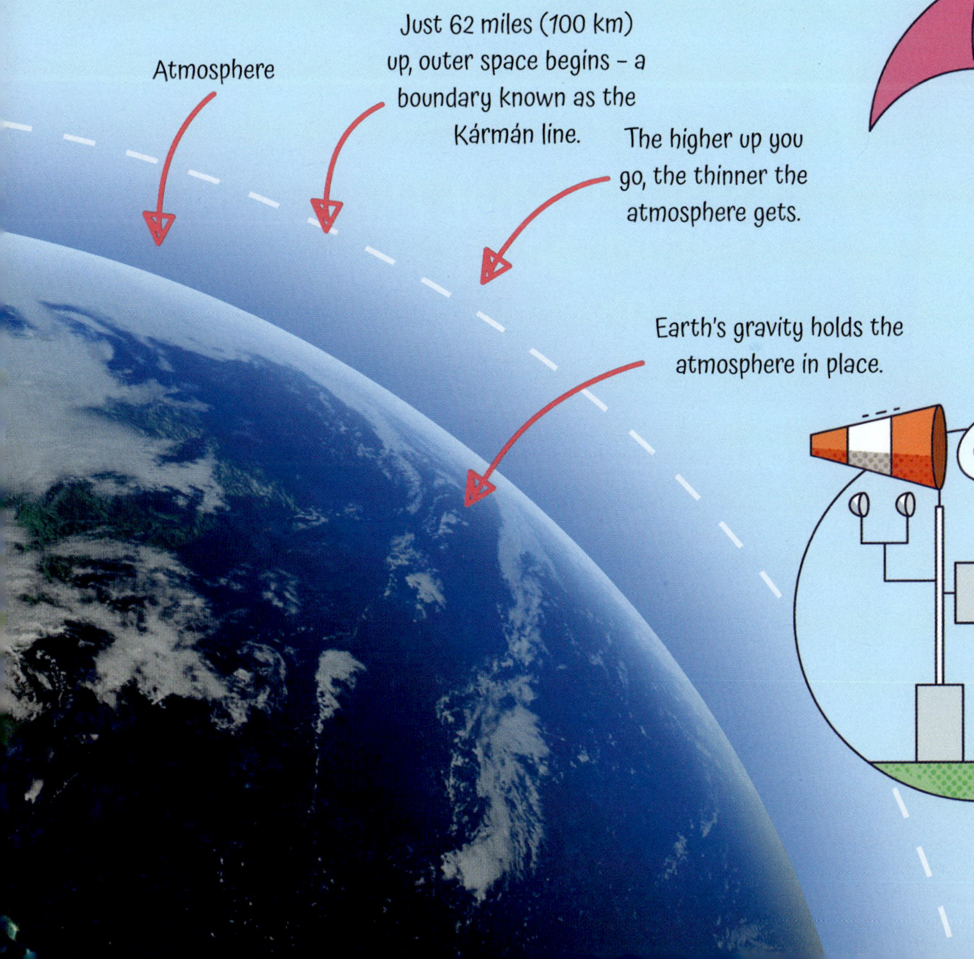

Atmosphere

Just 62 miles (100 km) up, outer space begins – a boundary known as the Kármán line.

The higher up you go, the thinner the atmosphere gets.

Earth's gravity holds the atmosphere in place.

THE SCIENCE OF WEATHER

The science of weather is called meteorology. But meteors are bits of space rock that burn up in the Earth's atmosphere, also known as shooting stars. What do they have to do with weather?

Meteorology gets its name from Aristotle's weather book, *Meteorologica*, dating from over 2,300 years ago. In ancient Greek, the word *meteoron* meant "something high up."

So Aristotle wasn't writing about meteors, but about what went on high in the sky. The name stuck and we still use it today!

METEORO-
= Stuff high up

+

LOGY
= study

WEATHER AND CLIMATE

WEATHER means what happens from day to day, such as a snow shower or a thunderstorm.

CLIMATE means general weather patterns or trends. For example, Mali in Africa has a mainly hot, dry climate.

Let's see what the weather has in store for tomorrow ...

Weather forecasting is also a huge part of weather science. That's because being able to predict the weather is so useful and important.

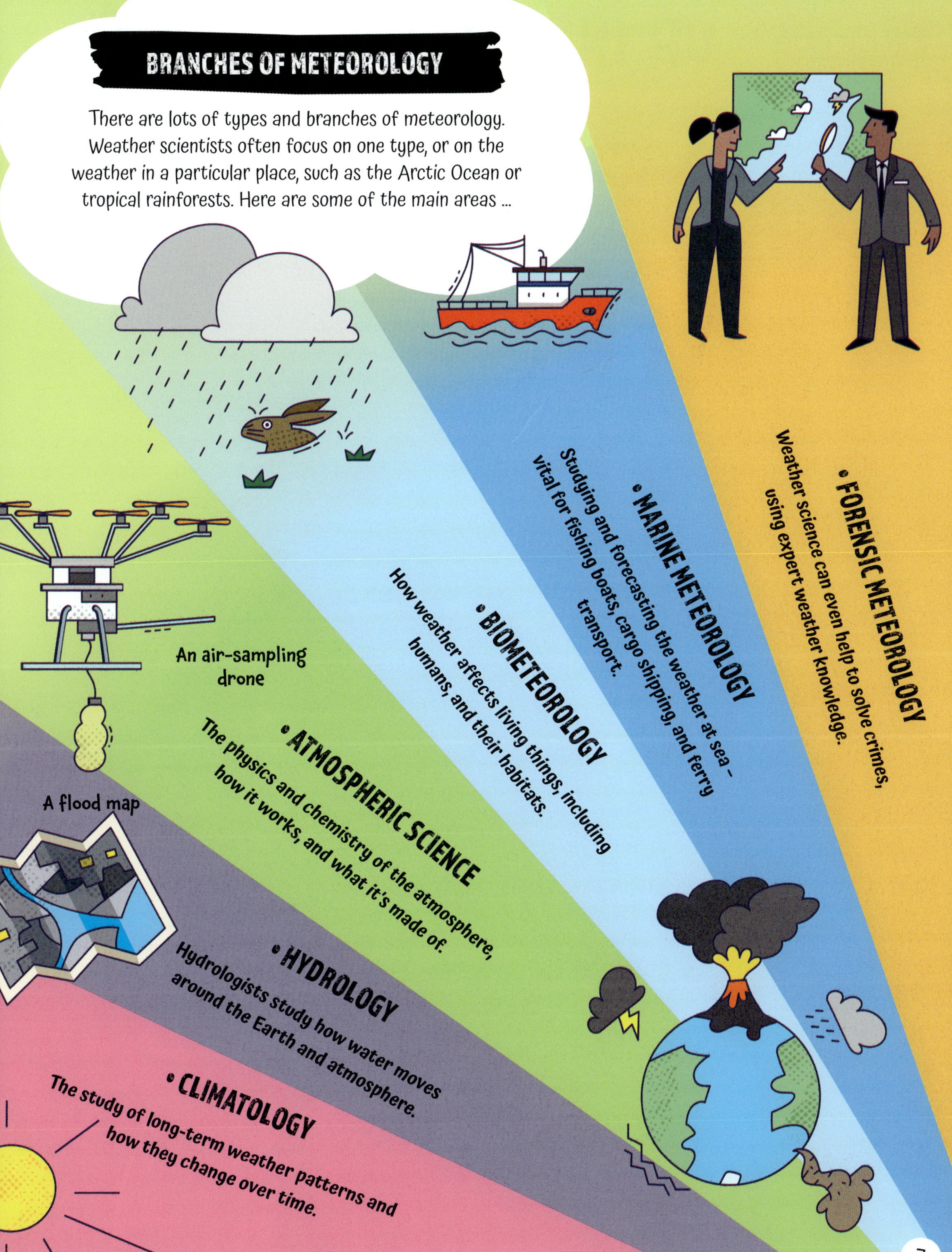

BRANCHES OF METEOROLOGY

There are lots of types and branches of meteorology. Weather scientists often focus on one type, or on the weather in a particular place, such as the Arctic Ocean or tropical rainforests. Here are some of the main areas ...

An air-sampling drone

A flood map

• FORENSIC METEOROLOGY
Weather science can even help to solve crimes, using expert weather knowledge.

• MARINE METEOROLOGY
Studying and forecasting the weather at sea – vital for fishing boats, cargo shipping, and ferry transport.

• BIOMETEOROLOGY
How weather affects living things, including humans, and their habitats.

• ATMOSPHERIC SCIENCE
The physics and chemistry of the atmosphere, how it works, and what it's made of.

• HYDROLOGY
Hydrologists study how water moves around the Earth and atmosphere.

• CLIMATOLOGY
The study of long-term weather patterns and how they change over time.

UP IN THE AIR

Weather happens in the atmosphere, so understanding the atmosphere is an essential part of weather science.

Layers of the atmosphere

When early hot-air balloonists tried flying as high as they could, they found the air got colder and colder the higher they went. But in the early 1900s, meteorologists used weather balloons with no one on board that could fly even higher – and discovered something surprising. The atmosphere had layers, and some of them were hot, not cold.

Today, scientists divide the atmosphere into these main layers:

Beyond the thermosphere, the outermost layer, the exosphere, fades away into space.

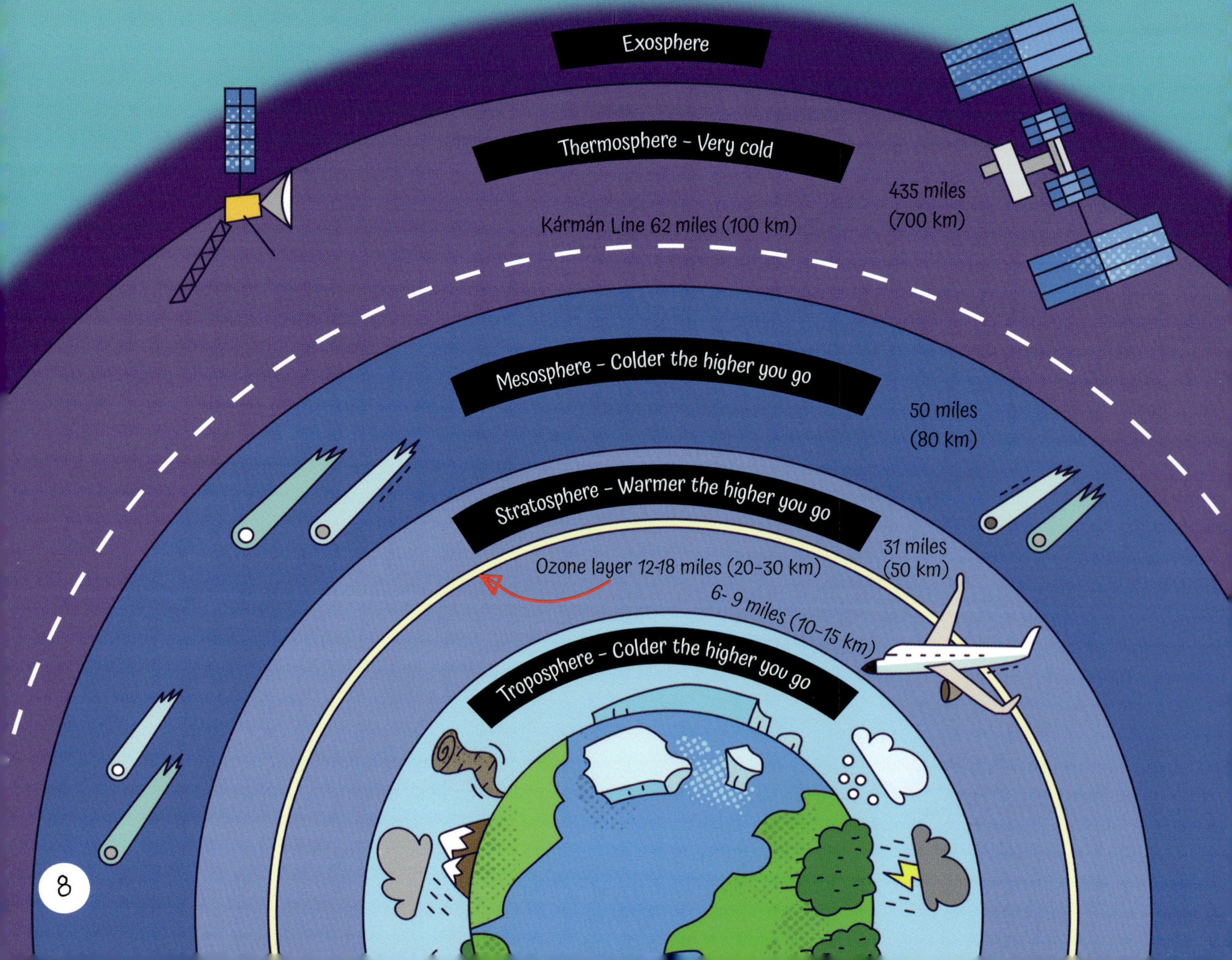

The birth of weather balloons

In 1902, two meteorologists, Léon Teisserenc de Bort in France and Richard Assmann in Germany, began using balloons to carry weather-measuring devices high into the sky, and discovered the stratosphere. Weather balloons are still used in meteorology today.

An early balloon flight to study the weather.

In the troposphere

The troposphere is the layer closest to Earth's surface, where the air is thickest. This air can hold the most water. So it's here that the water cycle happens, moving water from the sea and land into the air, where it then falls back down as rain or snow.

View from above

Today, meteorologists use weather satellites in space to detect things like the amount of moisture, or humidity, in the troposphere, to help predict the weather.

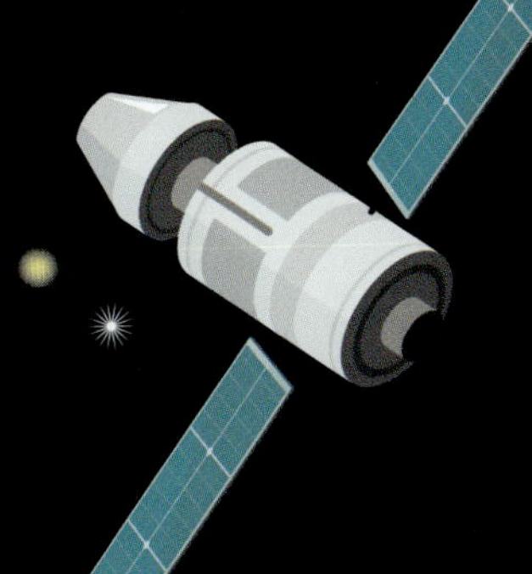

HIGHS AND LOWS

Weather forecasters often mention highs and lows – but what do they mean? They're talking about air pressure.

Under pressure

Air pressure, or atmospheric pressure, is a measurement of how much the atmosphere is pressing on the Earth. All the time, the weight of the atmosphere is pushing on the ground and on us. We just don't notice it because we're used to it.

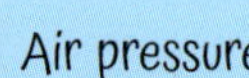

High and low pressure

Atmospheric pressure is always changing slightly as air heats up, cools down, and moves around. Here's how it works:

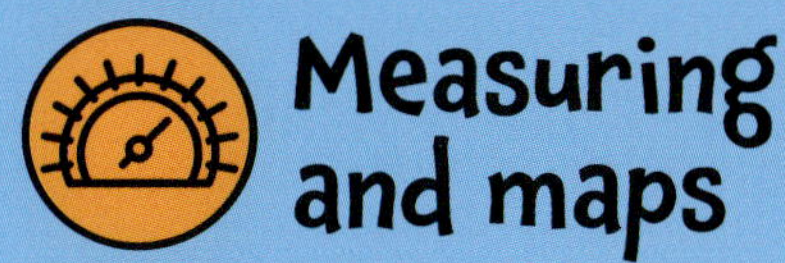

Measuring and maps

Meteorologists measure air pressure in millibars (mb) using a device called a barometer. The average air pressure at sea level is around 1013 mb.

Meteorologists collect pressure data from barometers all over the world to use in weather maps.

On a weather map, pressure is shown using lines called isobars.

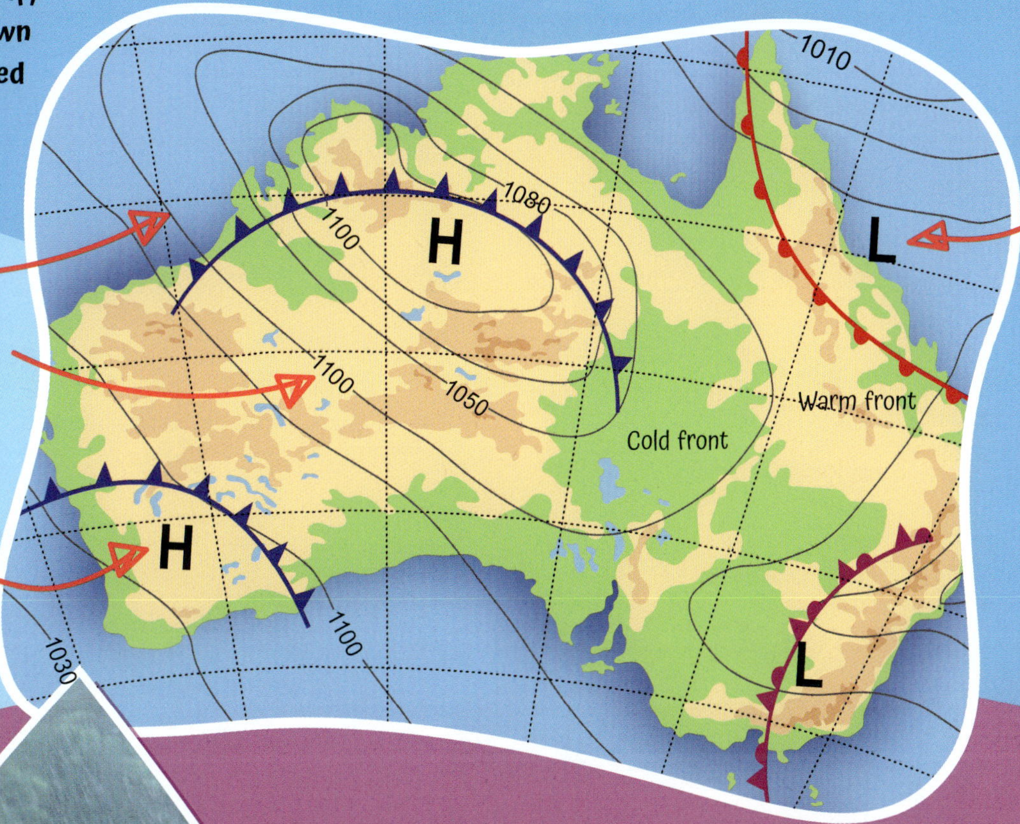

Isobar

Everywhere along this isobar has the same pressure, 1100 mb

A high, or high-pressure area

A low, or low-pressure area

High pressure usually means calm, settled weather. The sinking air warms up and spreads out along the ground. It doesn't form clouds, so the skies are usually clear and sunny.

Low pressure usually means unsettled weather, rain or storms. As the warm air rises, more air moves in along the ground to replace it, causing wind. The rising air cools, and the water in it forms clouds, leading to rain.

WEATHER STATIONS

Weather stations are places where special weather instruments record and measure weather data.

What are they like?

Weather stations come in a huge variety of shapes and sizes ...

The smallest type is just a simple mast with weather-measuring equipment attached to it ...

... while the biggest can take up whole buildings, like this one in Ukraine.

Farms and airports often have their own weather stations to help them plan and operate safely.

Where are they?

There are thousands of weather stations all over the world, including out at sea, so that meteorologists can track and monitor the weather everywhere.

The world's highest weather station is at 27,657 feet (8,430 m) above sea level, about 1,300 feet (400 m) below the summit of Mount Everest.

What they measure

A weather station has sensors to monitor different aspects of the weather, such as temperature, rainfall, and air pressure. At some stations, meteorologists check the instruments and report the readings hourly or daily. Many others are automatic. They're connected to the internet and upload their data to meteorology labs.

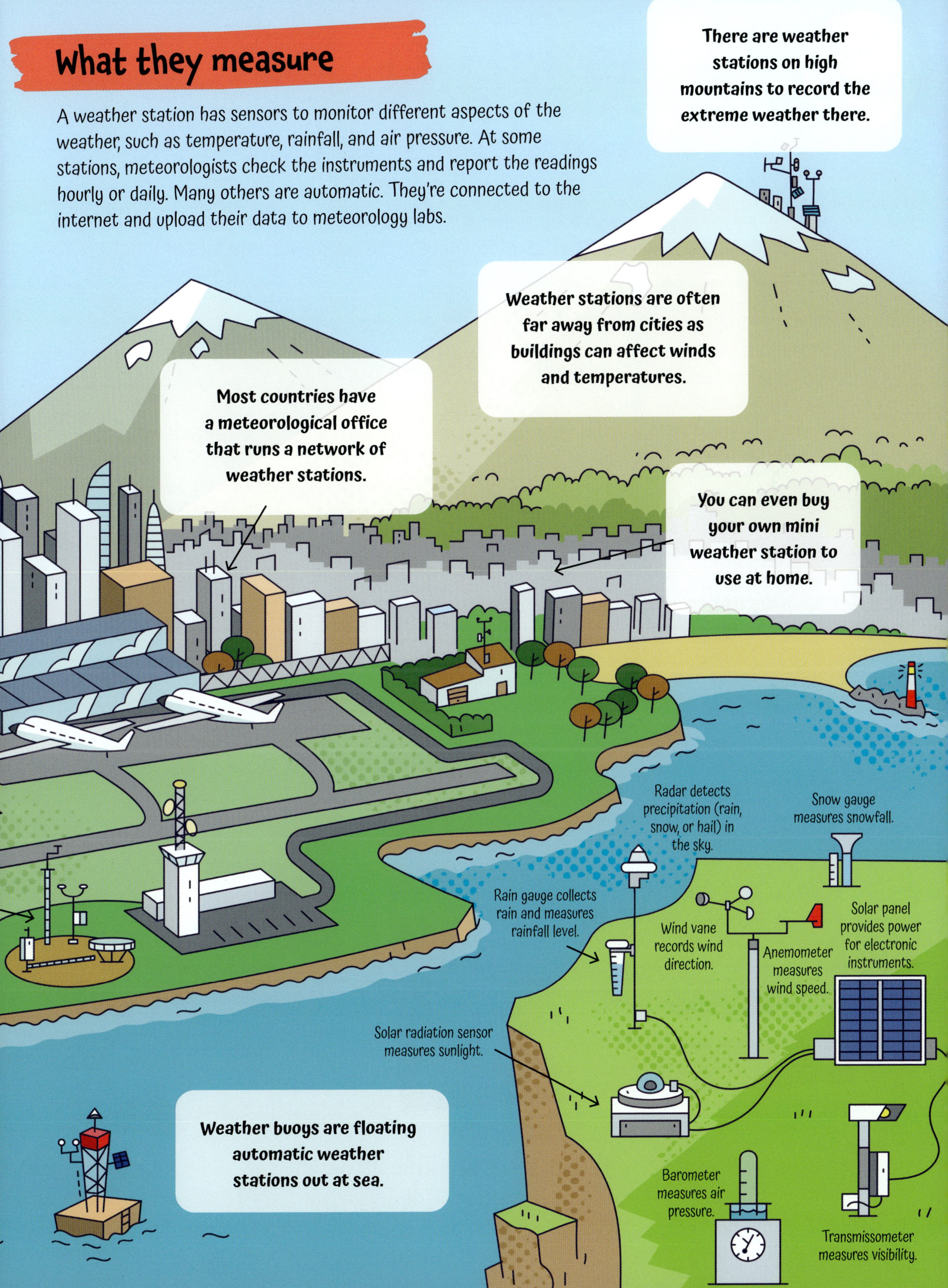

Willis Island weather station

It's the ultimate destination for a meteorologist: a tiny tropical island, with nothing on it but a hi-tech weather station, more meteorologists, and lots of wildlife!

Desert island

Willis Island lies in the Coral Sea, 280 miles (450 km) off the coast of Queensland in north-eastern Australia. It's just 1,640 feet (500 m) long by 490 feet (150 m) wide.

In 1921, Australia's weather forecasting office, the Australian Bureau of Meteorology (ABM), set up a weather station on Willis Island to spot cyclones (powerful windstorms) heading towards the Australian mainland and send an early warning. A hundred years later, it's still there!

Willis Island from the air

The island's wildlife includes seabirds, turtles, and crabs.

Island life

Willis Island weather station has four staff members–three meteorologists and a technical officer. They stay on the island in six-month shifts, then swap with someone else. The ship that takes them to and from the island also brings grocery supplies. There's a desalination plant to turn sea water into drinking water, a wind and solar power supply, and space for up to 10 visitors, as well as the four workers.

FACT FILE

DAILY ROUTINE

So what do the meterorologists do in a typical day? Their tasks include:

- Launching weather balloons every day, to measure weather data high in the atmosphere.
- Taking readings from the weather station radar equipment, and sending data to the ABM.
- Cleaning the equipment, which gets covered in droppings from all the island's wild seabirds.
- Fixing equipment damaged by salt water in the air.

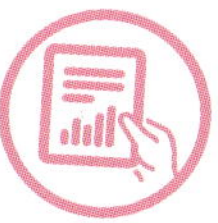

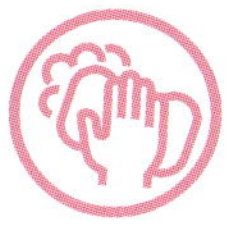

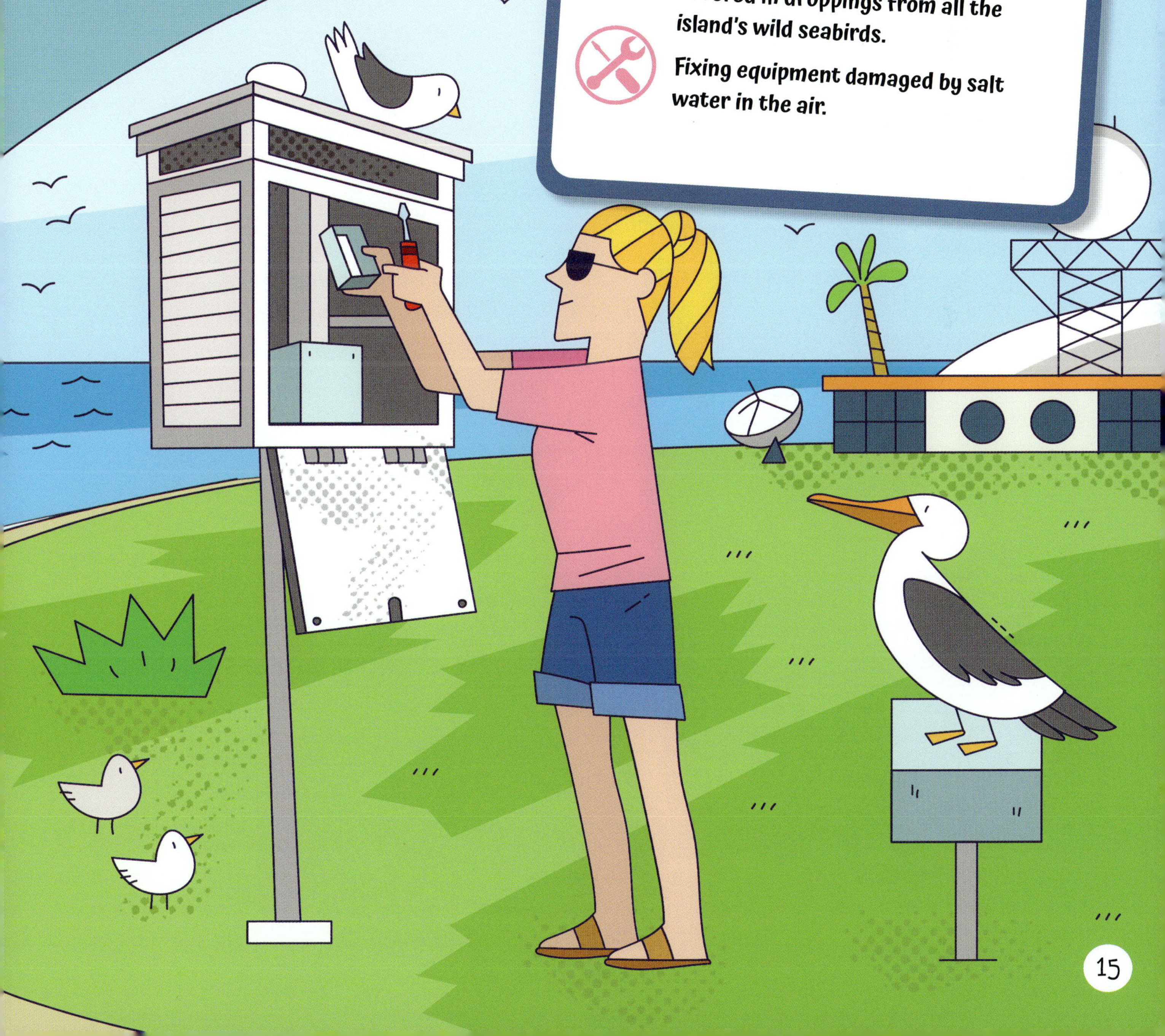

FLYING HIGH

Most weather happens in the troposphere (see pages 8-9), close to the Earth's surface. But there are interesting things going on higher up too.

Glaisher and Coxwell in their balloon basket, fitted with weather-testing equipment.

Jet streams

In the 1860s, English meteorologist James Glaisher and his co-pilot Henry Coxwell flew a balloon higher than ever before, reaching 32,800 feet (10,000 m) above sea level. They discovered a high-speed air current, flowing eastwards above Great Britain. And later, in the 1920s, Japanese meteorologist Wasaburo Oishi found that high-altitude weather balloons were blown eastwards by a powerful wind.

These scientists had discovered a jet stream, a giant air current that circles around the planet, caused by Earth's rotation. Today, we know much more about how the air in the atmosphere swirls and flows around in huge currents.

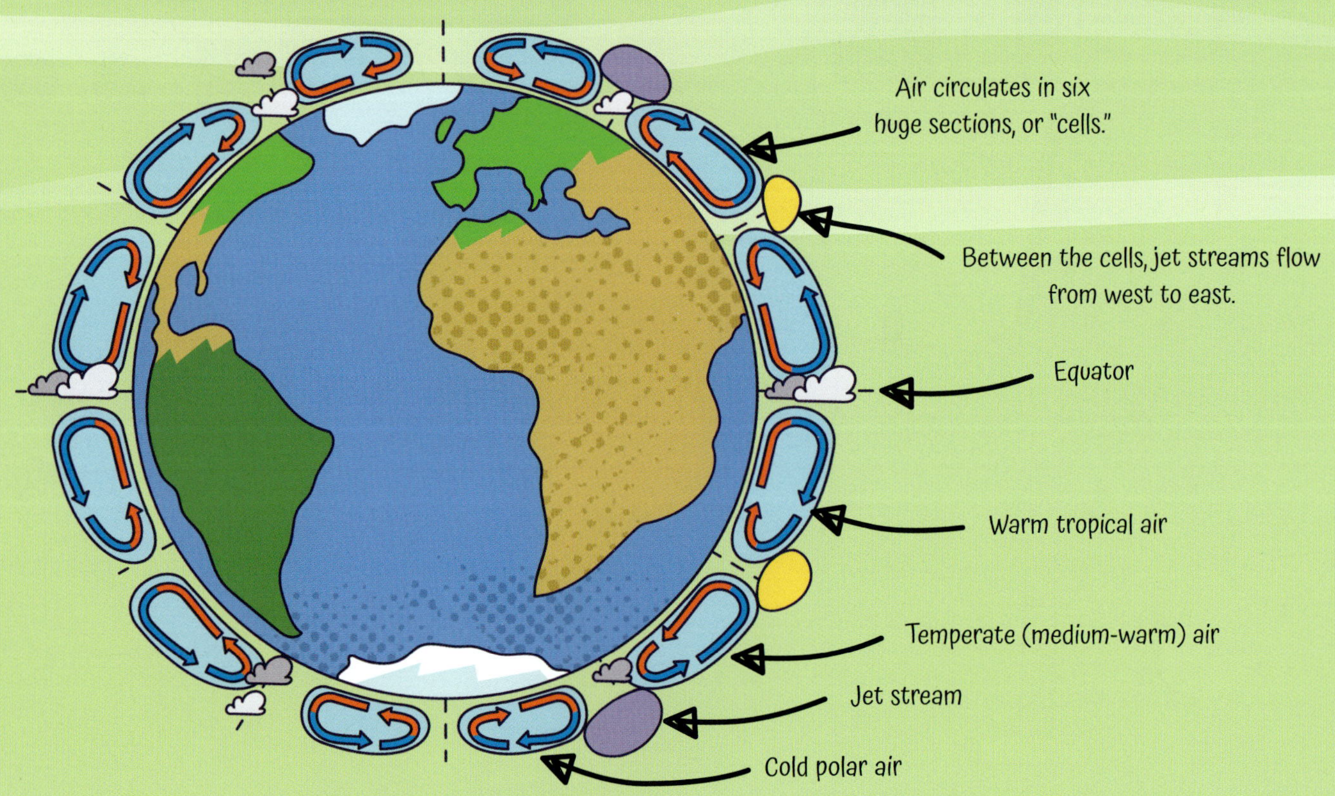

Changing the weather

Cells and jet streams stay roughly in the same places, but can change shape and move north or south, affecting how warm or cold the weather is in different places. Keeping track of jet streams is especially important for weather forecasting.

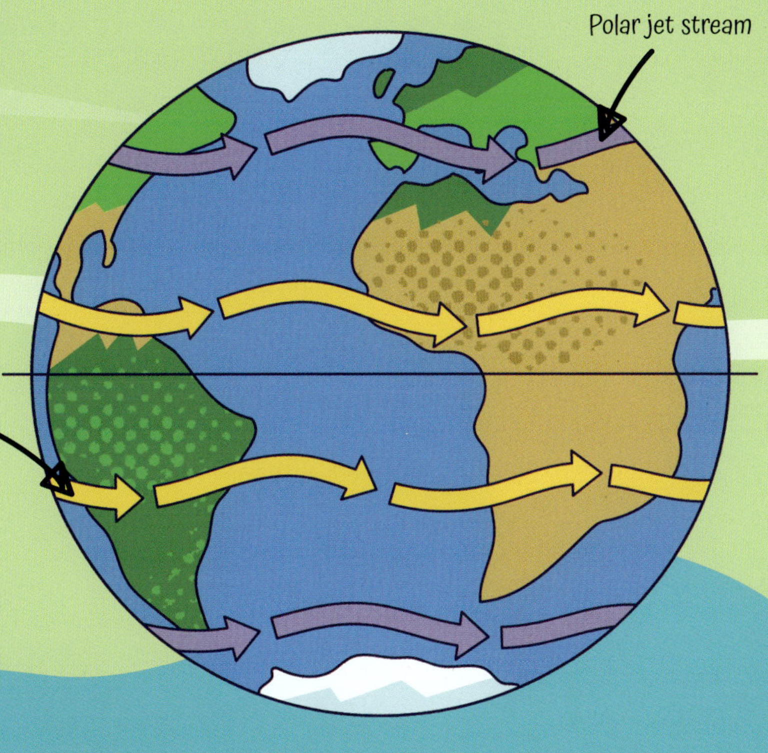

6.5 feet
(2 m) across

Up, up and away!

Meteorologists use weather balloons to collect weather data high in the sky. So how do they work?

Made of stretchy latex

Filled with lighter-than-air hydrogen or helium gas to make it float upwards

Parachute

Radiosonde, a box containing weather sensors and a radio transmitter to send data.

As it climbs higher and the air pressure drops, the gas expands, making the balloon grow several times bigger.

Eventually it bursts, and the radiosonde falls back to Earth on its parachute.

WHAT GOES UP, MUST COME DOWN...

Some radiosondes are never found, but others are recovered and reused. The balloon itself can cause litter pollution, so scientists are now developing biodegradable balloons.

SPACE SATELLITES

Near and far

There are two types of weather satellite.

Geostationary satellites orbit far out in space, about 22,300 miles (36,000 km) above Earth.

They orbit at the same speed as Earth rotates – so they stay over the same spot.

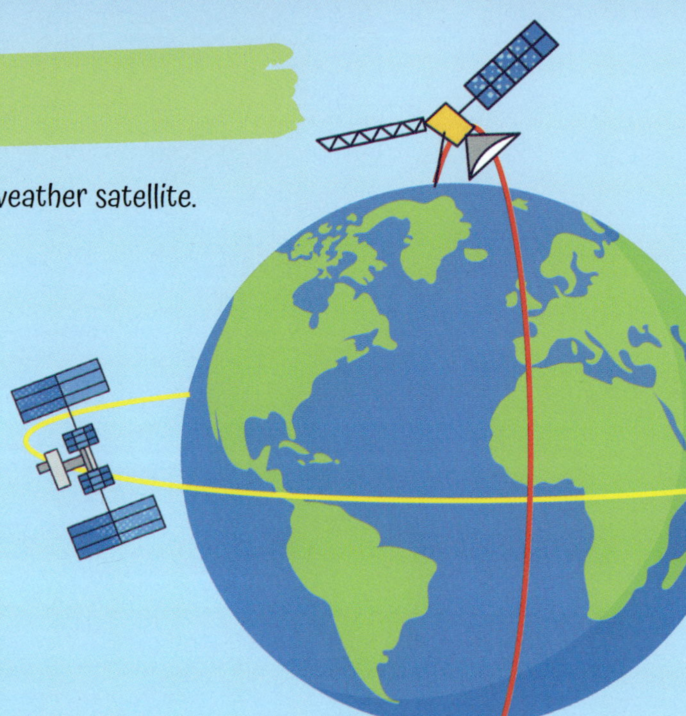

Polar satellites orbit around Earth in line with the poles.

They're closer, about 500 miles (800 km) above Earth. They scan the whole world as it rotates under them.

WHAT DO SATELLITES SEE?

Weather satellites collect several kinds of weather data:

- Land temperature, using an infrared sensor to detect heat
- Sea temperature, which can show where cyclones might form (see pages 20–21)
- Water vapor in the air, using a different wavelength of infrared
- Cloud cover, using digital cameras and telescopes
- Ice cover on the polar regions and glaciers
- Some weather satellites also collect data beamed up from weather buoys.

Collecting the data

Weather satellites constantly scan Earth for data and beam it down to the surface.

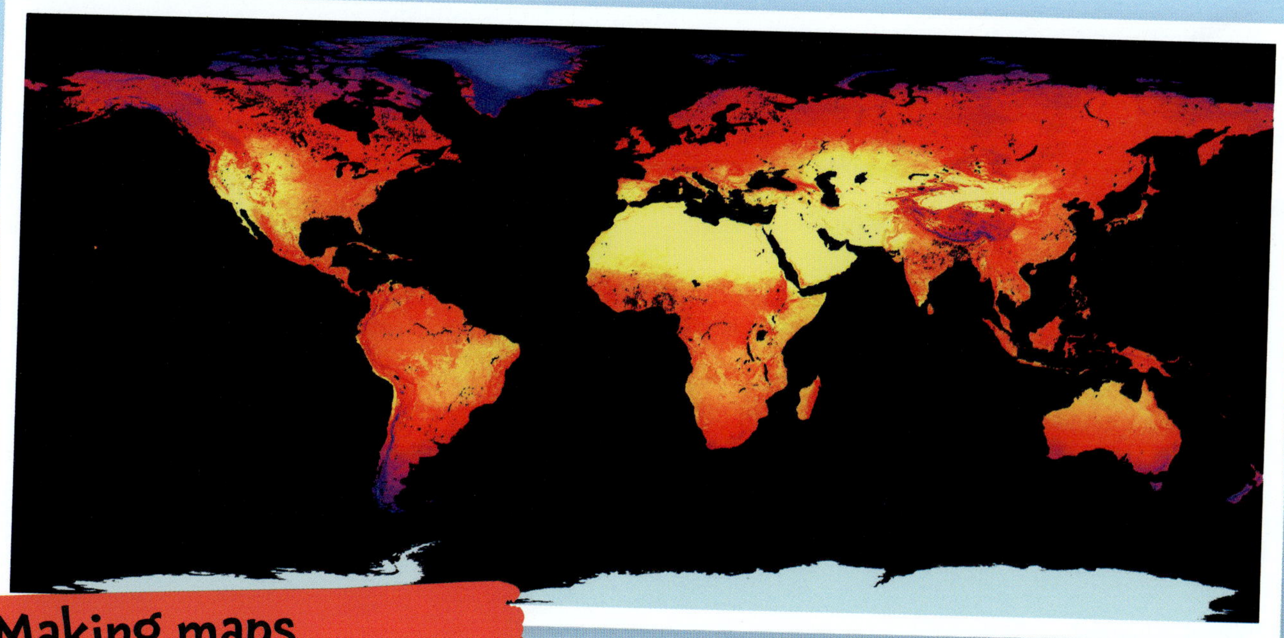

This satellite map shows Earth's surface temperature in August 2021.

Making maps

On the ground, meteorologists use computers to process the satellite data and turn it into maps. They can also make videos, showing how temperatures change or clouds move over time, helping to predict what will happen next.

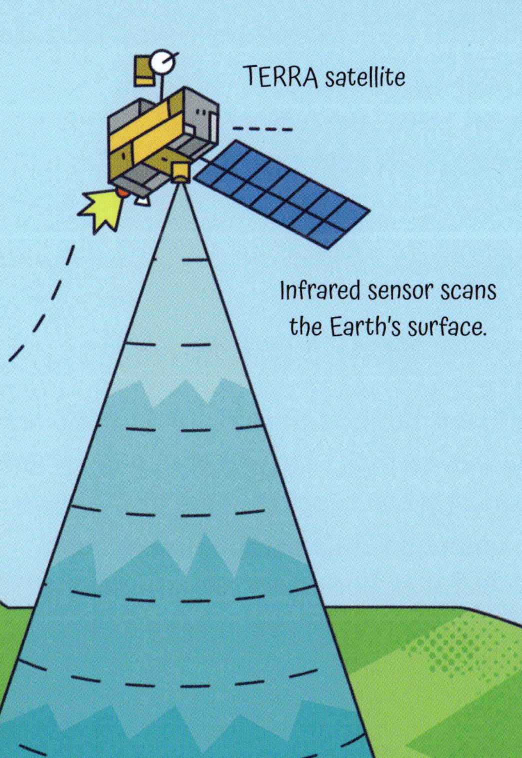

Satellite scientists

Besides working with data from satellites, some meteorologists help to design, build, and test new satellites and satellite weather sensors.

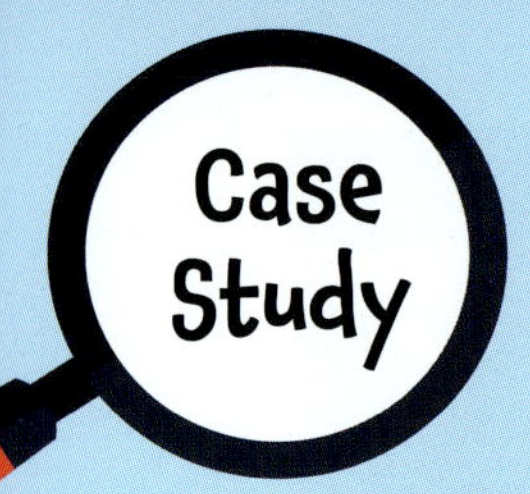

Typhoon alert!

When Typhoon In-fa formed over the Pacific Ocean in July 2021, meteorologists used satellite data and maps to predict its path.

What is a typhoon?

Typhoons are giant, whirling, rainy windstorms, also known as cyclones or hurricanes, depending where in the world they are. Meteorologists call them tropical cyclones.

Winds and clouds form a huge spiral that swirls across the ocean.

Typhoons form over warm oceans, when warm, wet air rises up, cools, and forms clouds. The low pressure sucks in more damp air.

Spotted out at sea

On July 16, 2021, satellites detected a storm forming near the Pacific island of Guam. By July 19, it was big enough to be classed as a typhoon. Images captured by the TERRA weather satellite showed it heading for Japan, the Philippines, and China.

WHAT'S IN A NAME?

Meteorologists give tropical cyclones names to make them easy to describe in weather reports. This storm was named Fabian in the Philippines, but was known as In-fa (meaning "fireworks") around the world.

Typhoon In-fa passing over southern Japan and approaching China on July 21, 2021.

Where is it going?

Using data from satellites and weather stations, weather forecasters could predict the path of the typhoon and show where it was likely to hit land, bringing gales, heavy rain, and flooding.

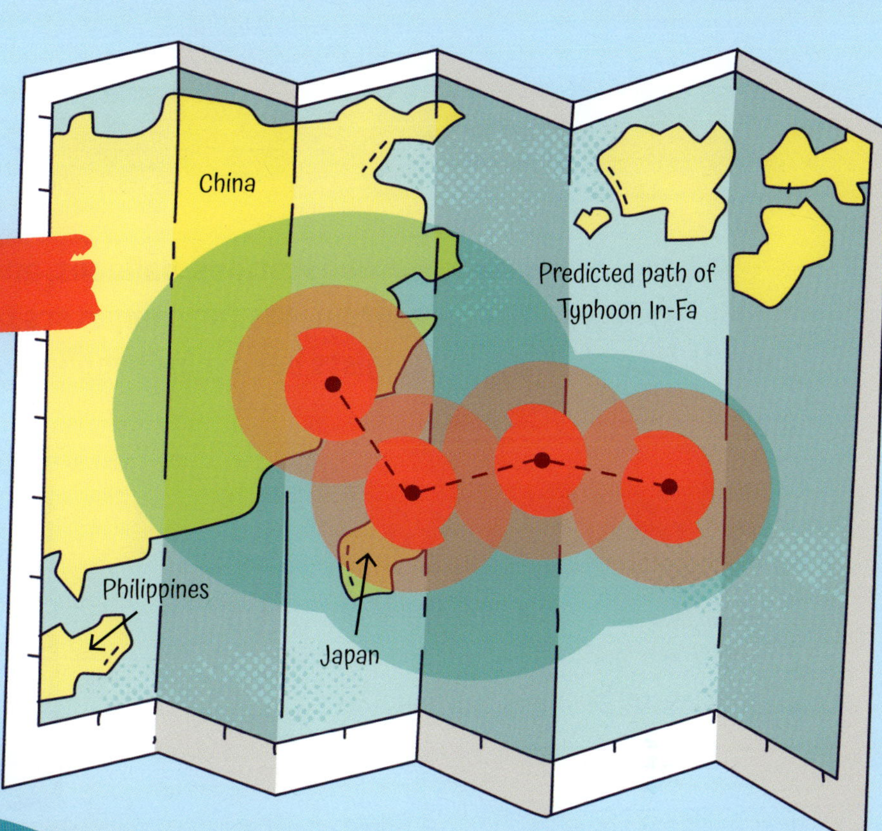

Storm incoming ...

As the typhoon approached, people were evacuated from their homes, flights and trains were canceled, and some events at the Tokyo Olympics were rescheduled. Ships headed into harbor to shelter, and dams and reservoirs were drained so they didn't overflow.

In-fa caused severe flooding and landslides, blew down trees, and damaged houses. Several people sadly died – but it would have been much worse without the advance warning from meteorologists.

FACT FILE

TYPHOON IN-FA

FORMED: JULY 16, 2021

SIZE: 500 MILES (800 KM) ACROSS

FASTEST WINDS: 108 MILES (175 KM) PER HOUR

COST OF DAMAGE: OVER $ 2 BILLION

COMPUTER POWER

All day, every day, weather stations, balloons, and satellites collect millions of weather measurements for computers to process. There's SO MUCH data that meteorologists need mindbogglingly powerful computers.

Top of the FLOPS

Meteorologists use supercomputers, which are much bigger and faster than normal computers, to process or "number crunch" data.

A home or office computer could have four processor cores, which do calculations, and work at 1 teraFLOPS — that's a trillion (1,000,000,000,000) calculations per second.

Sounds like a lot!

But a weather supercomputer could have 100,000 cores and work at 10 petaFLOPS.

A petaFLOP is a quadrillion (1,000,000,000,000,000) calculations per second — making the supercomputer 10,000 times faster.

Because they contain so many processors, weather supercomputers are HUGE. This shows part of one.

What do they do?

Supercomputers use weather data to make models, or simulations, of weather systems.

The computer creates a 3D grid to map out the space and all the data from each place.

Making it work

While some meteorologists use the models to make maps and forecasts, others work as computer scientists. They design and write the software for the supercomputers, or even design and build the supercomputers themselves.

Keep your cool!

Supercomputers get very hot while doing all those calculations, so they have liquid flowing around inside them to cool them down — a bit like a fridge.

To work with supercomputers, you have to be brilliant with computers, but also know a lot about weather and how it works.

Then, using mathematical calculations, it "fills in" the gaps between all the data points.

Then, the computer can "run" the model, simulating the weather changing over time, and use all the data to show what will probably happen next.

For example, if the data shows two different temperatures in two nearby locations, the computer will work out what it must be in between.

MAKING MODELS

Every day, supercomputers model whole weather systems to make forecasts. But meteorologists can also make smaller models, to help them study particular places or different types of weather.

In a computer

Computer models or simulations are one way to do this. They let you recreate a weather event, then slow it down and study what's happening, or experiment with changing things like the temperature or humidity.

Inside a twister

Tornadoes are high-speed, deadly windstorms, and we need to forecast them to save lives. But they're also hard to understand, and dangerous to get close to.

So meteorologists have made tornado computer models, that can "replay" a tornado and show how it works inside – like this one created at the University of Wisconsin.

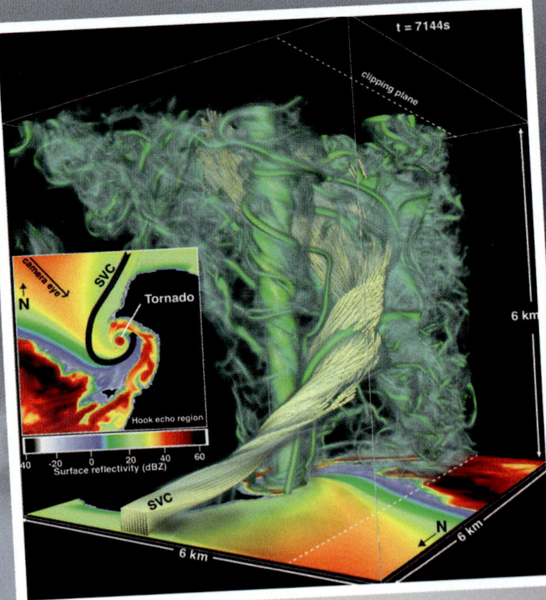

The model shows how different streams of hot and cold air meet and swirl around inside the tornado, and how it grows and gets stronger.

This lab at Iowa State University has a large tornado-making machine and a little model town to test it out on!

Real-life models

Sometimes, meteorologists also make real, physical models to recreate weather events.

For example, they can recreate hurricanes and tornadoes in miniature in a lab, using smoke or dry ice. You can sometimes see storm simulators in museums too.

FACT FILE

HOW BIG IS YOUR MODEL?

Meteorologists study and model the weather at several different scales, or sizes, which have different names. They are:

GLOBAL SCALE
The whole world, or something Earth-sized, such as a jet stream.

SYNOPTIC SCALE
Large weather patterns thousands of miles in size, such as a hurricane system.

MESOSCALE
Medium-sized weather patterns, such as a local thunderstorm.

MICROSCALE
Small, local weather events, such as how wind flows around a building.

MORE MODELS

All kinds of weather events can be studied using a model ...

Can you think of more?

What do you think would be a good way to model each of these things?

MAKING MAPS

It's often very useful to show weather on a map. There's not just one type of weather map, though. You can use them to show all kinds of things.

Science research

When meteorologists find something out about the weather, they often use maps to illustrate their results. A map can show things at a glance that would take much longer to explain.

This is an anomaly map, used to illustrate climate change. Anomaly means "different from normal."

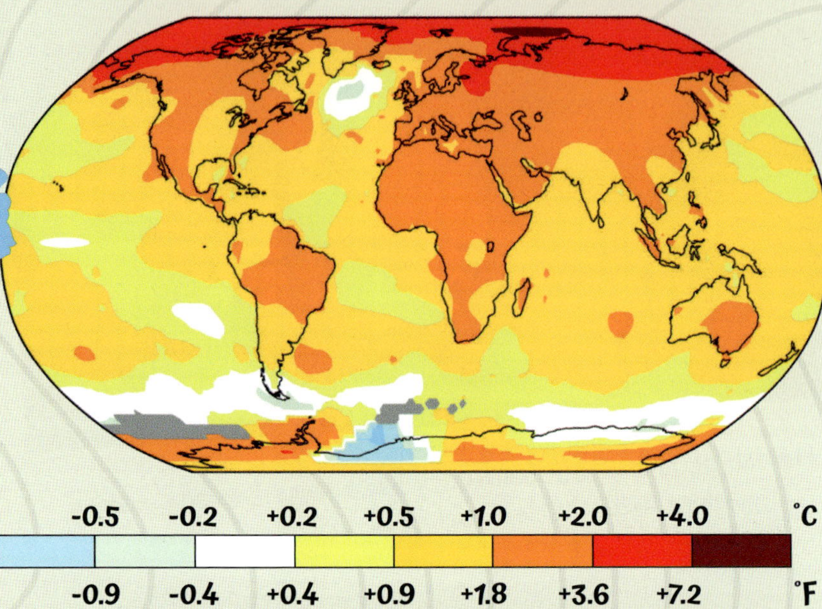

It doesn't simply show temperatures. Instead, it shows if the temperature in a particular year or time period was higher or lower than the average. Yellow, orange and red mean higher, and blue means lower. As you can see, due to global warming (see pages 34–35), it's mainly getting higher.

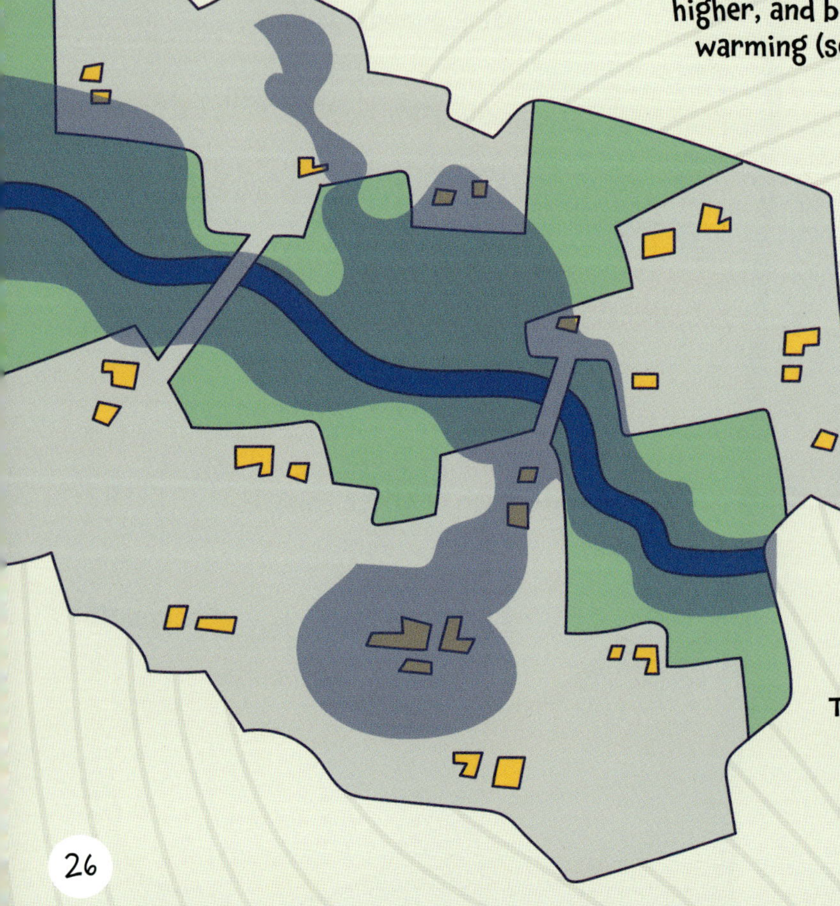

? What could happen?

Another type of map acts like a model to predict what would happen in a particular situation. For example, which parts of a city or country will flood after heavy rain? This information could be useful for lots of people, such as house builders, house buyers, and insurance companies.

The blue shading on the map shows the areas that are most likely to flood if heavy rain makes the river overflow.

Forecast maps

Weather forecasts use several different types of map to show different things – because if they were all on the same map, it would be too confusing. Maps can show temperature, clouds, wind patterns, air pressure (see page 10), or ice and snow on the ground.

This weather forecast map shows different types of weather, including clouds, rain, and sunshine.

MAPPING SOFTWARE

Long ago, people had to draw maps carefully by hand. Today, they're mostly made on computers, using GIS (Geographic Information System) software, which turns data into a map on the screen. GIS can also make animated maps that change over time.

WEATHER FORECASTING

As this book shows, a LOT of work goes into predicting the weather: collecting data, crunching it in a supercomputer, and making maps. Finally, it's ready to become a finished weather forecast.

• Weather broadcasts on TV have a presenter and animated maps.

• In weather bulletins on the radio the forecast has to explain everything clearly in words, as there is no map to look at.

• Weather maps and information are printed in newspapers …

… and posted on news websites and weather apps.

The general public

Who needs a weather forecast?

Weather forecasts come in different forms depending on who needs them and why.

Farmers

Special farming forecasts cover things that affect crops and animals, such as frost and droughts. These are available on the internet, and on the radio early in the morning.

Ships and sailors out at sea

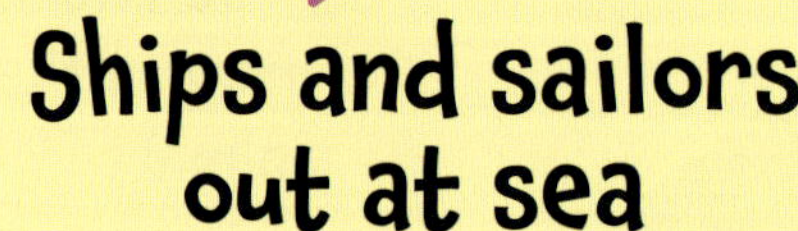

Shipping forecasts broadcast by internet and radio, to help boats avoid storms and fog.

Space scientists

They need detailed weather info to help them study the stars or launch rockets!

To make a weather forecast, someone has to turn the science-y information and maps into easy-to-understand versions.

• Designers and artists make clear, stylish maps for TV and newspapers.

• Writers explain the forecast in simple, friendly language. For example, a weather scientist might talk about "precipitation," but a forecast writer would probably change that to rain or snow.

Weather symbols

British scientist Francis Galton (1822-1911) invented the first weather symbols in 1861, to show different types of weather on a map – and they're still used today.

In early TV weather forecasts, the presenter stuck little stickers onto the map!

Cloudy with sunny spells

Light rain

Today, the symbols appear on the map as part of a computer graphic.

Heavy rain

Here's a modern set of weather symbols.

Can you tell what the rest mean?

Snow

In the studio

Every day, thousands of TV weather forecasts are broadcast all around the world. Take a look behind the scenes to see how they work ...

Presenters and maps

When you watch a TV weather forecast, you usually see a weather presenter standing in front of a big map, which they point to as they talk.

But did you know there's often no map there at all? In most forecasts, the presenter actually stands in front of a "green screen." Computer software then adds the map to the green area, so it looks as if it's behind the presenter.

Making a forecast

Here's how it works ...

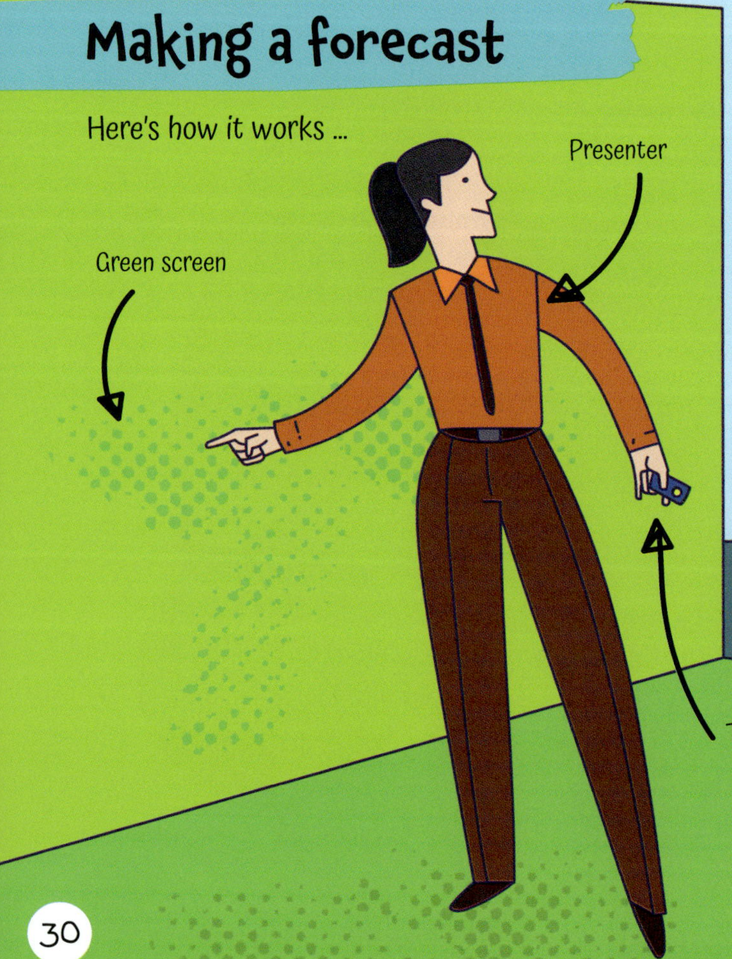

The presenter uses a small remote control to change to the next map.

Weather presenting skills

Some weather presenters are trained in TV skills, but are not weather scientists. They present a weather report that meteorologists prepare for them. Others are meteorologists who help to put together the weather report before they present it.

Either way, presenting the weather is a skilled job, especially if it's live! You have to:

- **Talk about the weather in a way that's easy to understand.**

- **Keep it friendly, chatty, and interesting.**

- **Look relaxed and speak confidently into the camera.**

- **Stick to a strict time slot, and stop talking at exactly the right moment.**

- **Stay cool and keep chatting if something goes wrong!**

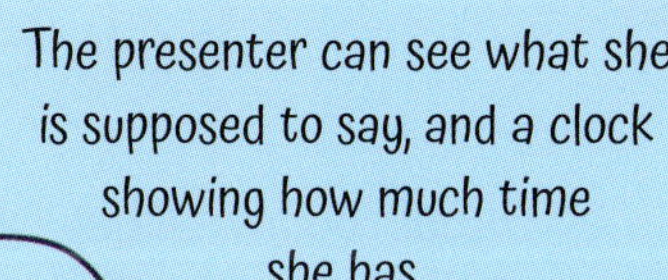

The presenter can see what she is supposed to say, and a clock showing how much time she has.

Camera films the presenter talking about the weather.

She can also see herself on a monitor with the map added, so she knows where to point.

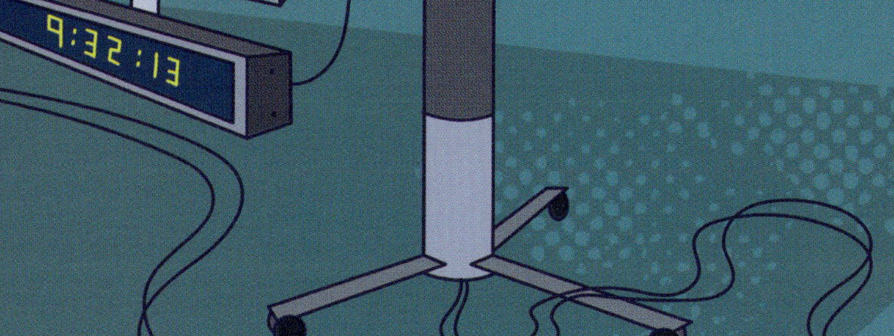

NO GREEN, PLEASE!

A green screen map will appear anywhere that looks green — so weather presenters can't wear green clothes!

DANGER AND DISASTERS

Weather can be deadly. In fact, some of the worst natural disasters in history have been caused by weather – and even everyday weather is sometimes dangerous and destructive.

• Lightning strikes

Lightning strikes kill around 2,000 people around the world each year.

• Fog

Thick fog makes it hard to see, sometimes causing car and plane crashes.

• Tornadoes

These small but super-powerful windstorms destroy buildings and throw cars into the air.

It's scary out there!

Dangerous weather ranges from huge floods and heatwaves that kill thousands of people, to slipping on an icy pavement. Here are some examples ...

• Hurricanes, typhoons, and cyclones

These massive windstorms damage buildings and bring heavy rain and flooding.

• Landslides

Soil and rock soaked with rain slip downhill, landing on roads or houses.

Severe weather warning!

We can't prevent dangerous weather – at least not yet! (See page 42.) But meteorologists play a big part in keeping people safe by studying it, forecasting it, and providing safety advice. In fact, meteorologists have probably saved millions of lives.

• Heatwaves

Extra-hot weather causes illness when people overheat and dehydrate, and can also lead to wildfires.

Sometimes, meteorologists themselves face dangerous situations to find out more about weather. One example is storm chasing: trying to get close to thunderstorms and tornadoes to study them.

• Floods

Caused by heavy rain, big waves, or melting ice and snow.

• Ice storms

In an ice storm, cold rain freezes onto surfaces in thick layers, pulling down trees and power lines, and causing car crashes on slippery roads.

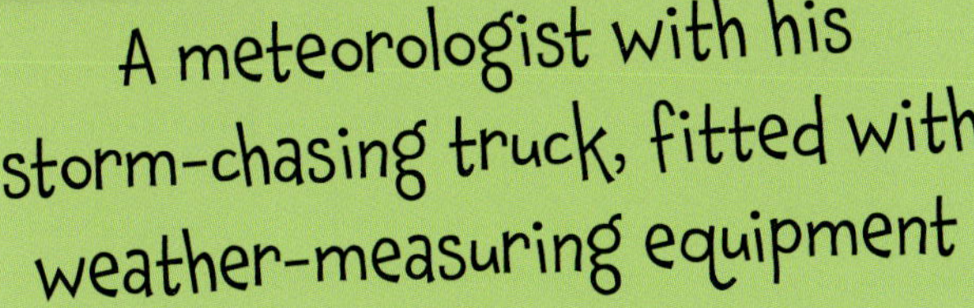

A meteorologist with his storm-chasing truck, fitted with weather-measuring equipment

CLIMATE CHANGE

It's one of the biggest topics for meteorologists, and for everyone else too. The world is warming up, and its weather and climate are changing, due to human activities.

? What happened?

Over the past 200–300 years, humans have started using many new inventions, such as factory machines, cars, planes, and electrical gadgets. To power them, we've burned more and more fossil fuels, such as oil, coal, and gas.

This releases waste gases into the air, especially carbon dioxide, or CO_2. This "greenhouse gas" helps to trap heat from the sun in Earth's atmosphere. When there are more greenhouses gases in the air, Earth warms up – a process known as global warming. We've been studying how this works since the 1800s.

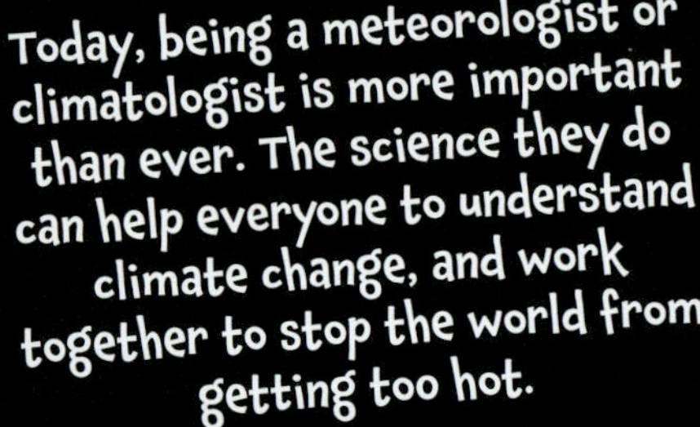

In 1856, American scientist Eunice Foote experimented with bottles of air and carbon dioxide, and found that the CO_2 heated up more in the sun.

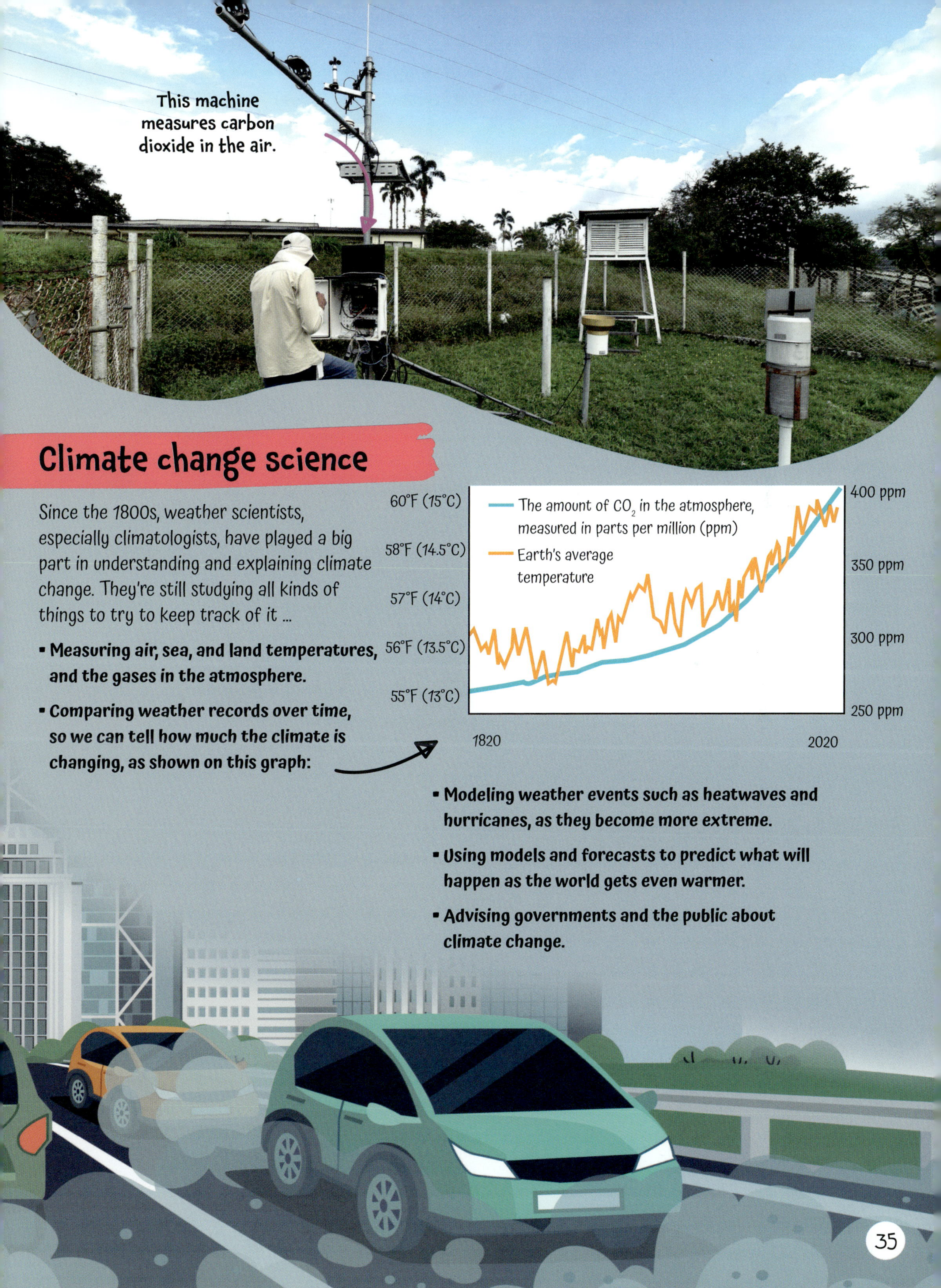

Climate change science

Since the 1800s, weather scientists, especially climatologists, have played a big part in understanding and explaining climate change. They're still studying all kinds of things to try to keep track of it ...

- **Measuring air, sea, and land temperatures, and the gases in the atmosphere.**

- **Comparing weather records over time, so we can tell how much the climate is changing, as shown on this graph:**

- **Modeling weather events such as heatwaves and hurricanes, as they become more extreme.**

- **Using models and forecasts to predict what will happen as the world gets even warmer.**

- **Advising governments and the public about climate change.**

Out on the ice

How do we know what the climate was doing thousands of years ago? From ice cores – cylinders of solid ice, drilled out of deep ice sheets.

Ice history

Ice sheets are the huge blankets of ice covering Antarctica and most of Greenland. They are made of snow that has fallen over many centuries, and packed down into solid ice. As this happened, bubbles of air got trapped in the ice along with specks of dust, plant pollen, and volcanic ash.

The lower down the ice is, the older it is. In Antarctica, the deepest ice is over 2.7 million years old! So climatologists can find out about the atmosphere in the past by studying the ice and the things trapped in it.

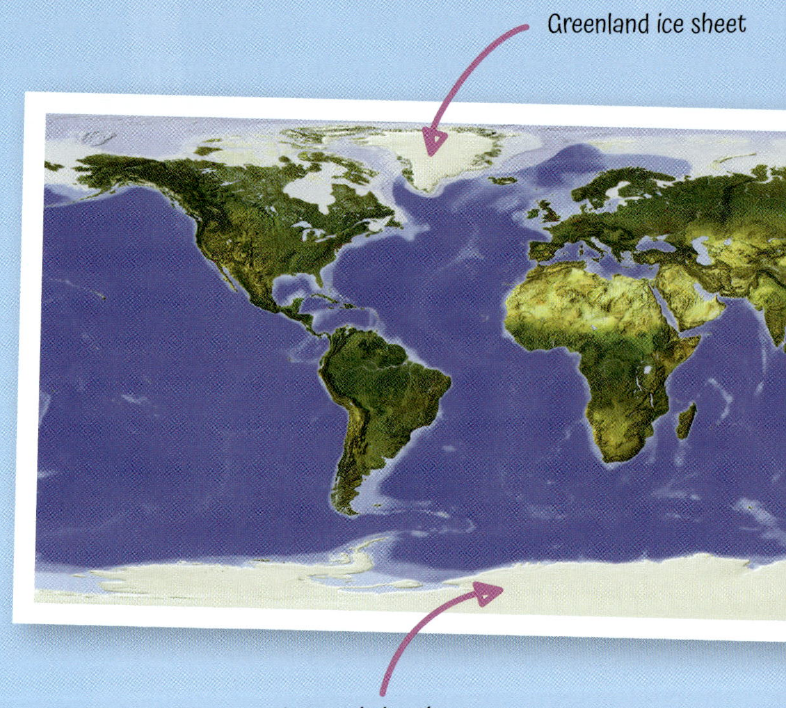

Antarctic adventure

To study ice cores, scientists have to stay on the ice sheet for days or weeks. They use a huge, powerful drill to bore as deep as 9,800 feet (3 km) down into the ice, and extract the ice cores.

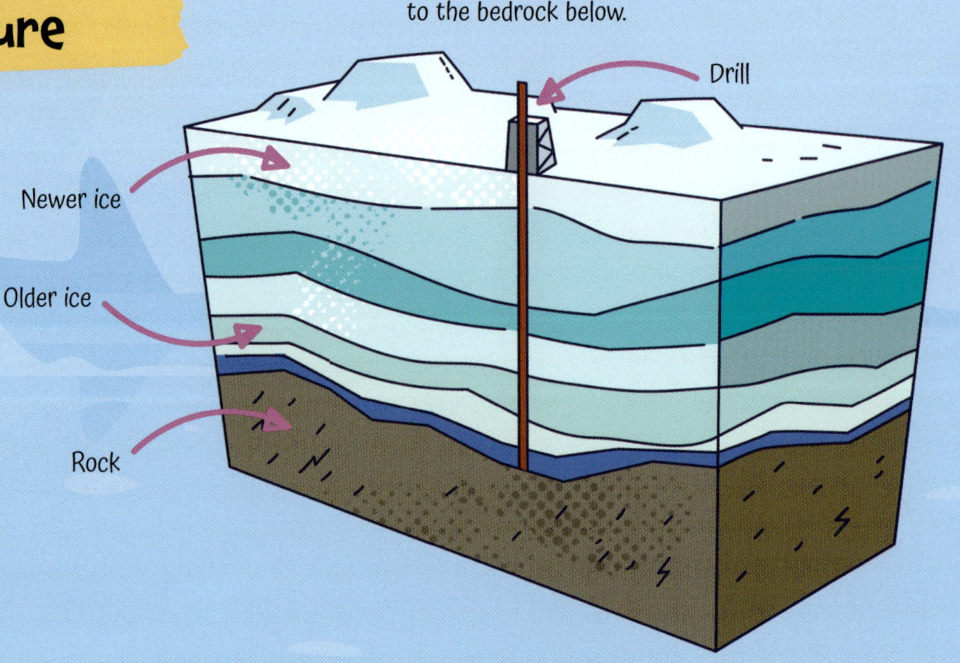

Secrets in the ice

Studying the ice cores is useful because it can show what happened when the climate changed long ago. Was there more carbon dioxide in the air then? How did warmer temperatures affect the air quality and living things such as plants? This can help us to understand the climate change that's happening now.

Working on the ice

Antarctica is one of the most extreme environments you can work in as a weather scientist. It's windy, bone-chillingly cold (with temperatures as low –112°F/–80°C) and far from any shops, cafes or towns.

Greenland isn't quite as cold and remote, but it has dangerous polar bears ...

This could be your home for weeks or months. Cozy!

THE EARTH'S ECOSYSTEM

Weather and climate are part of a bigger system – the global ecosystem. That means the Earth as a habitat, and all the plants, animals, and other creatures that live on it.

WHO STUDIES THIS?

Lots of scientists are studying the effects of weather and climate on life and ecosystems, especially the impact of climate change. They're often called ecological or environmental meteorologists (or climatologists), or biometeorologists.

The air we breathe

The gases in the air are constantly moving between the air and living things.

This means living things play a big part in balancing the different gases in the atmosphere. For example, trees absorb carbon dioxide from the air – so chopping down forests makes global warming worse.

Weather and living things

Weather affects living things in all kinds of ways, just as it affects our own lives. For example, a big storm could blow migrating birds off course, so they end up far from home. A flood could swamp animals' burrows, so they have to move somewhere else.

Climate change is making extreme weather events more common, as well as increasing temperatures around the world. This can change habitats and put some species at risk.

Climate change is also enabling some animals to live in new places, disrupting local ecosystems.

CORAL BLEACHING

Corals are tiny sea creatures that live in groups and build hard, shell-like coral around them. As seas get warmer, corals can become stressed and push out the algae that live inside them, give them their color, and help them survive. This "coral bleaching" makes them look pale, and eventually die.

A scientist goes diving to study coral bleaching in the Indian Ocean

WEATHERPROOF!

Throughout history, we've been inventing and making things to protect us from the weather, both low- and hi-tech.

Brilliant ideas

Some of these weather inventions date from ancient times, but they're still in use today.

Mists of time: Umbrellas

Providing protection from both sun and rain, umbrellas have been around for thousands of years. Even orangutans use them.

3,000 years ago: Asian conical hats

Asian conical hats are used in many Asian countries as protection from the sun and rain.

They are often made from woven plants and can be dipped in water to keep the wearer cool.

Structures and buildings

Meteorologists sometimes work on bigger projects too, such as flood shelters on stilts or giant flood barriers that keep land safe from flooding.

This flood barrier protects a low-lying area of the Netherlands from sea storm flooding.

1752: Lightning rod

Benjamin Franklin, an American scientist who studied lightning, came up with this genius invention. It's a metal rod fixed on top of a building to attract lightning strikes and carry the electricity safely down into the ground.

1976: GORE-TEX

Father and son, Wilbert and Bob Gore invented this waterproof fabric that stops rain but lets water vapor out, so you don't get sweaty.

FACT FILE

WHAT DO WE NEED NOW?

Because of climate change, we still need more inventions and solutions to protect people from extreme weather events and rising sea levels, such as ...

- Weather disaster warning systems
- Floodproof and windproof homes and other buildings
- Ways of keeping buildings, animals, and people cool without wasting electricity
- Ways of turning flooded areas into land we can build on.

CAN WE CONTROL THE WEATHER?

Since prehistoric times, people have tried to control the weather, by praying to weather gods or doing rain dances. But is it possible?

Whatever weather you want!

Imagine if we could completely control the weather. We could prevent weather disasters, give farmers the perfect conditions for their crops, and ensure sunny days for weddings, festivals, and holidays.

We're nowhere near being able to do all this. But we have a start, especially when it comes to making it rain.

This ancient rock art from southern Africa is thought to show people catching a "rain animal," possibly a hippo, to try to make it rain.

Many countries now use cloud seeding to make it rain on crops, or on areas hit by droughts, heatwaves, or wildfires. These Chinese weather office staff are firing rockets into the clouds to spread cloud-seeding chemicals.

Cloud seeding

Clouds form when water vapor in the air forms tiny water droplets. This happens when water vapor starts to condense onto specks of dust in the air. They collect together and get bigger, and eventually fall as rain.

So, in the early 1900s, weather scientists figured out that by adding more dust-like particles to clouds, we could make more water droplets, and turn clouds or humid air into rain – a process known as cloud seeding.

Speck of dust 

Water 

Raindrop 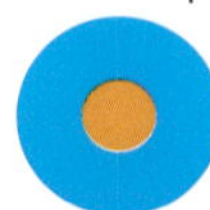

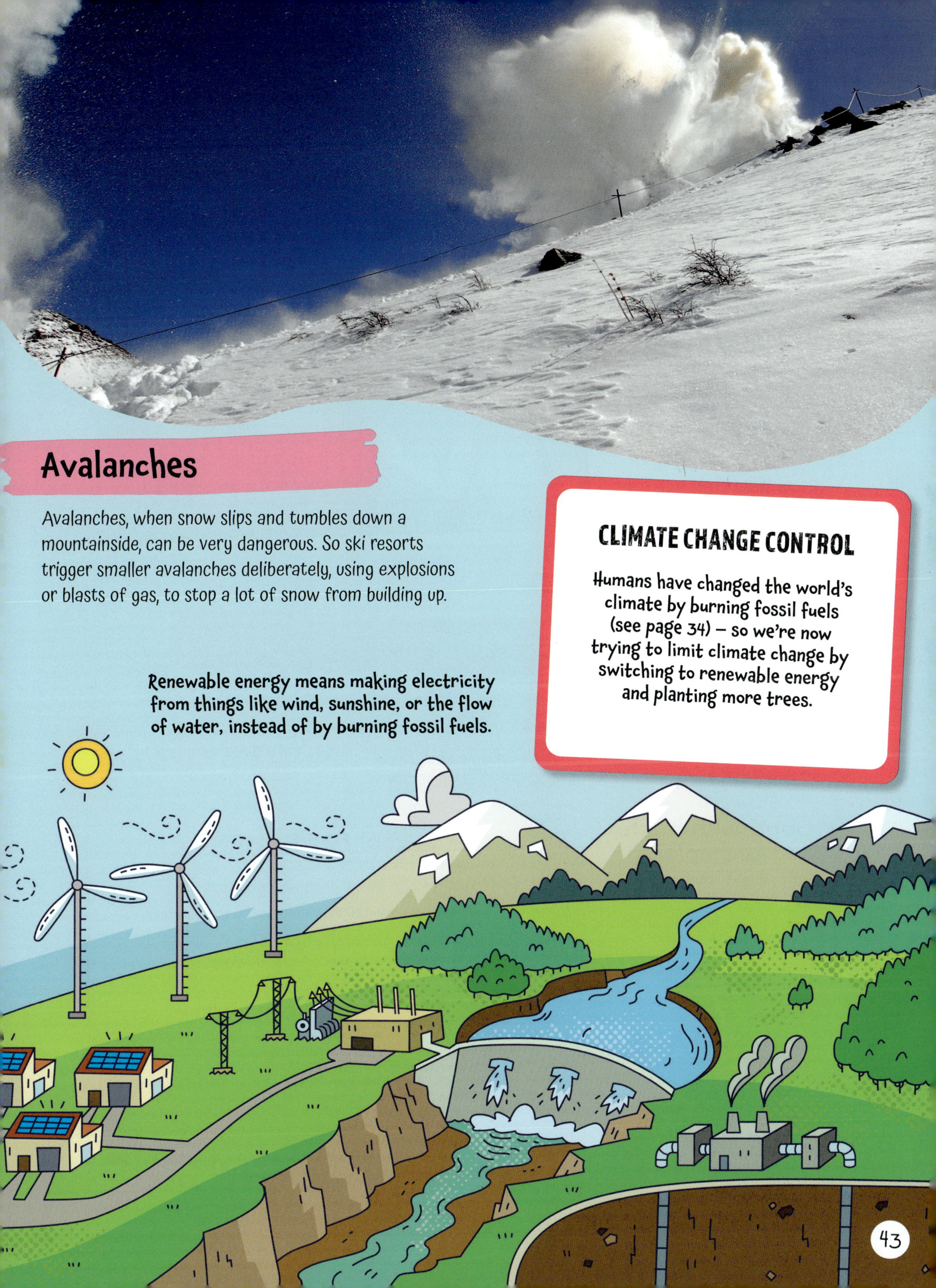

Avalanches

Avalanches, when snow slips and tumbles down a mountainside, can be very dangerous. So ski resorts trigger smaller avalanches deliberately, using explosions or blasts of gas, to stop a lot of snow from building up.

Renewable energy means making electricity from things like wind, sunshine, or the flow of water, instead of by burning fossil fuels.

CLIMATE CHANGE CONTROL

Humans have changed the world's climate by burning fossil fuels (see page 34) — so we're now trying to limit climate change by switching to renewable energy and planting more trees.

IS METEOROLOGY YOUR OLOGY?

Do you like the idea of being a meteorologist, climatologist, or weather forecaster? That's good, because we need weather scientists now more than ever before. But how do you make it happen?

What makes a good meteorologist?

Studying weather and climate is a huge area of science, and it can involve all kinds of different skills and abilities. So the most useful qualities depend on what you're doing – from climbing a rainforest tree to writing software or presenting a TV weather show. However, these interests and abilities are all good to have ...

• Good with math and technology

Many weather jobs involve calculating, figuring out predictions, and using computers. If you like math, science, and technology, that's a great start.

• A cool head

Whether you're clambering across a slippery glacier, launching a space satellite, or doing a live weather forecast, you need to stay cool, calm, and in control.

• Outdoorsy

Not all weather scientists work outdoors, but being a meteorologist can involve traveling to remote places, using skills like SCUBA diving or climbing, and of course, working in some wild weather conditions.

• Love the weather!

Do you find weather endlessly fascinating, and can't stop watching footage of floods and tornadoes? Are you concerned about climate change and eager to find solutions? Weather science needs you!

SUBJECTS TO STUDY

As you get older, you get to choose your favorite subjects to study in school.

These are all great options for budding weather enthusiasts ...

• **Math** is key to weather modeling and forecasting.

• **Computer science** is essential for working with weather supercomputers.

• **Physics**, **chemistry**, and **geography** are helpful to know.

• **English**, **drama**, **media studies**, **science communication**, or **journalism** could all be useful for TV weather forecasters, writers, and filmmakers.

• In college, you can study for a degree in **meteorology** – but **Earth science**, **computer science**, and other sciences can also lead to a weather career.

What else could you do?

Besides being an actual meteorologist, there are several other related jobs and activities:

• Climatologist

• Weather forecaster

• TV weather presenter

• Military and airline forecaster

• Researcher.

GLOSSARY

Air pressure Another name for atmospheric pressure.

Anemometer A device that measures wind speed.

Atmospheric pressure The way the atmosphere presses on us and on the Earth.

Avalanche A mass of snow sliding down a steep slope.

Barometer A device that measures air pressure.

Bedrock The solid rock underneath soil, sand, or other materials on the Earth's surface.

Biodiversity The variety of living things in a particular habitat, or in the whole world.

Blizzard A snowstorm that combines snow and strong winds.

Carbon dioxide A type of gas found in the air, which contributes to global warming.

Cells Huge rotating masses of air in the Earth's atmosphere.

Climate The typical or average weather in a particular place, or on Earth as a whole.

Climate change A long-term change in climate patterns.

Cloud seeding Releasing tiny particles into clouds or damp air to help rain to fall.

Cold front A place where a mass of cold air is moving forward and replacing warmer air.

Computer simulation A simulation, or copy, of a real-life thing or situation, programmed into a computer to help scientists to study it.

Condense To change from a gas into a liquid.

Cyclone A swirling windstorm around an area of low air pressure. Also used to mean a tropical cyclone in the Indian or South Pacific Ocean.

Drought A period of very dry weather that can cause water shortages and harm crops.

Ecosystem A habitat and the community of living things that are found there.

Environment The surroundings, especially natural surroundings or the natural world .

Fog A thick cloud of water droplets in the air at ground level.

Fossil fuels Fuels such as oil, coal, and gas, which formed from ancient living things.

Front The front edge of a moving mass of air.

Frost A layer of ice caused by water vapor freezing onto freezing cold surfaces.

Gale A strong wind.

GIS (Geographic Information System) A computer system that collects and displays data about geography or the Earth.

Glacier A large slow-moving mass of ice on a mountain or in a polar area.

Global warming A gradual increase in Earth's average temperature over the last two centuries, caused by human activities.

Greenhouse gases Gases, such as carbon dioxide, that trap heat in the Earth's atmosphere, leading to global warming.

Habitat The natural home or surroundings of a living thing.

Hail Balls or pieces of ice that fall in showers, usually during thunderstorms.

Heatwave A period of unusually hot weather, usually during the summer.

High An area of high atmospheric pressure.

Humidity The amount of water vapor in the air or atmosphere.

Hurricane A tropical cyclone In the Atlantic or northeastern Pacific Ocean.

Ice core A cylinder of ice drilled out of a glacier or ice sheet.

Ice sheet A very big and long-lasting layer of ice covering an area of land.

Ice storm A build-up of ice on the ground, buildings, and objects, caused by rain freezing onto ice-cold surfaces

Infrared An invisible type of light energy.

Isobar A line on a weather map that shows a particular level of atmospheric pressure.

Jet stream Fast-flowing air currents that flow around the Earth, around 5-8 miles (8-13 km) above the ground.

Kármán line An imaginary line 62 miles (100 km) above Earth's surface, used to mark the division between Earth and space.

Landslide Soil or rocks sliding or slipping down a slope.

Low An area of low atmospheric pressure.

Meteorologist A scientist who studies weather and the atmosphere.

Millibar A unit of measurement, used to measure atmospheric pressure.

Modeling Making a model of a real-life situation or thing to help you study it.

Oxygen A gas found in the air, which animals need to breathe in.

Ozone layer A layer of the atmosphere containing a lot of ozone, a type of oxygen.

Precipitation Water that falls from the atmosphere to the ground, such as rain, snow, or hail.

Radiosonde An instrument that measures weather data and transmits the results using radio signals.

Rain gauge A device that measures the amount of rainfall.

SCUBA (short for Self-Contained Underwater Breathing Apparatus) Diving underwater with an oxygen supply carried on your back, so that you can breathe.

Snow gauge A device that measures the amount of snow that falls.

Solar radiation sensor A device that measures the amount and strength of sunshine.

Species The scientific name for a particular type of living thing.

Storm chasing Following thunderstorms and tornadoes to study or photograph them.

Tornado A powerful windstorm that forms a narrow spiral or funnel of whirling air.

Transmissometer A device that measures visibility in the atmosphere.

Tropical Used to describe the warm parts of the Earth on either side of the equator.

Tropical cyclone A large, spiral-shaped windstorm that forms over warm tropical oceans. It can also be called a hurricane, cyclone, or typhoon.

Typhoon A tropical cyclone in the northwestern Pacific Ocean.

Warm front A place where a mass of warm air is moving forward and replacing colder air.

Water vapor Water in the form of a gas, which makes up part of the atmosphere.

Weather balloon A type of balloon with measuring devices on it that is released into the sky to measure weather conditions.

Weather buoy A floating instrument that collects weather and ocean data at sea.

Weather satellite A human-made satellite orbiting the Earth, used to capture images of weather patterns or record weather information.

Weather station A building or device that measures many different aspects of the weather.

Wildfire A fire burning out of control across a large area, especially in the wilderness or countryside.

Wind vane A device that shows the direction of the wind.

Further information

BOOKS

Forecasting the Weather
by Marie Harts (Britannica Educational Publishing, 2025)

Weather and Climate
by Doris Wargula (Britannica Educational Publishing, 2025)

Wild Weather
by Fabiola Sepulveda (Teacher Created Materials, 2025)

WEBSITES

NASA Climate Kids
Information about all kinds of climate and weather topics, including how space satellites collect weather data.
climatekids.nasa.gov/menu/weather-and-climate

NOAA National Severe Storms Laboratory
All about the most extreme storms, winds, ice, and other extreme weather.
www.nssl.noaa.gov/education/svrwx101

Science Kids: Weather
Lots of weather facts, photos, cool videos, experiments, and activities.
www.sciencekids.co.nz/weather.html

Note to parents and teachers: every effort has been made by the Publishers to ensure websites are suitable for children, that they are of the highest educational value, and that they contain no inappropriate or offensive material. However, because of the nature of the internet, it is impossible to guarantee that the contents of these sites will not be altered. We strongly advise that internet access is supervised by a responsible adult.

INDEX

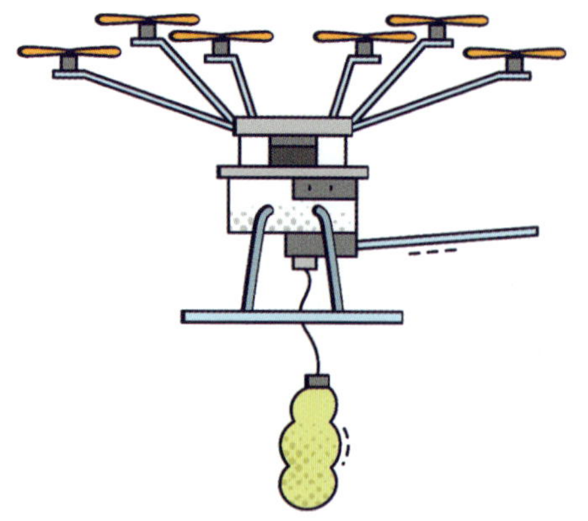